BEYOND 2.0

THE FUTURE OF MUSIC

STEVE COLLINS AND SHERMAN YOUNG

SHEFFIELD UK   BRISTOL CT

Published by Equinox Publishing Ltd.

UK: Office 415, The Workstation, 15 Paternoster Row, Sheffield, South Yorkshire, S1 2BX
USA: ISD, 70 Enterprise Drive, Bristol, CT 06010

www.equinoxpub.com

First published 2014

British Library Cataloguing-in-Publication Data
A catalogue record for this book is available from the British Library.

Library of Congress Cataloging-in-Publication Data
Collins, Steve (Stephen David), author.
  Beyond 2.0 : the future of music / Steve Collins and Sherman Young.
    pages cm. -- (Music industry studies)
  Includes bibliographical references and index.
  ISBN 978-1-84553-938-2 (pbk.)
  1. Music trade. 2. Music and technology. I. Young, Sherman, author. II.
Title.
  ML3790.C665 2014
  338.4'778--dc23
                        2013038390

ISBN: 978 1 84553 938 2   (paperback)

Typeset by CA Typesetting Ltd, www.publisherservices.co.uk
Printed and bound in the UK by Lightning Source UK Ltd., Milton Keynes and
Lightning Source Inc., La Vergne, TN

Contents

Introduction

The Oscar-winning film *The Piano* (1993) tells the story of Ada, who emigrates from her native Scotland to distant New Zealand, accompanied by her daughter and her beloved piano. The drama centres on Ada's sense of loss (and then sexual awakening) after her new husband discards the piano. Set in the late 1800s, *The Piano* reminds us that there was a time when people's relationship to music was dramatically different from our contemporary experience. Little over a century ago, music meant live performance; even in a domestic setting, the prerequisite for enjoying music was not only the presence of an instrument (for the most part a piano) but someone with the ability to play that instrument. This was also true at a social level – the communal music experience was one of live performance, with a small group of performers entertaining a larger audience in a concert-hall or music-hall setting.

The introduction of new recording and broadcasting technologies as the twentieth century dawned enabled a dramatic shift. Not only did it reshape the social experience of music, but it also, over time, resulted in an economic model for industrialization that came to dominate and in turn shaped a new musical culture. With the ability to produce and distribute a recorded artefact, the technologies of the phonograph and radio allowed the eventual displacement of the domestic performance prerequisite. Subsequently, the role of the live musical experience shifted to a supporting one   for professional musicians, concert tours became promotional tools, which generated sales of recorded music. Over the course of a hundred years, the role of live performance was displaced. Aside from childhood music lessons, it largely disappeared from the domestic context as professionally performed music became more easily accessible via radio and recorded artefacts.

Instead, live performance shifted from the drawing room to the stage. Professional and amateur musicians turned to a kind of theatrical performance in a range of public, rather than private, venues. In the twentieth century, Ada's piano went from being a commonplace centrepiece of domestic entertainment to an occasional presence used only for the stumbling scales of a child's music practice. Just as machines had significantly enabled the reshaping of other social, cultural and economic practices, the early twentieth century brought an industrialization of music that would shape how music was produced and consumed for much of that century. (It is worth noting, however, that childhood music practice continues to this day – and probably still provides the foundation for many of the musicians who will grow up and form the basis of that industry.)

We have noted this prehistory of twenty-first-century music to better contextualize current conversations about the contemporary state of music – or more accurately the music industry. Such discourses can tend to privilege existing paradigms and suggest that the late-twentieth-century environment where music production and distribution were dominated by a handful of "majors" is a natural state of affairs. This book contends otherwise. Just as new technologies afforded the twentieth-century industrialization of music, the impact of contemporary media technologies (digitization, the multimedia computer and the internet) has afforded a re-industrialization. And the current contests are better understood as part of a continuum of change during which human engagement with music (at both an individual and social level) has constantly evolved.

Music, as with most other media forms, is in the middle of a period of enormous transformation. Digital technologies have empowered producers and consumers of music; accepted ways of making and distributing music are under threat as musicians and their audiences embrace new opportunities, many of which bypass the incumbent middlemen. The changes are so dramatic that the term "Music 2.0" is now commonly used to distinguish the old music from the new. We use that term in this book, not to suggest revolution (as some have done) but as shorthand – a means to describe the changes afforded by those new technologies. We are aware that the term Music 2.0 might appear somewhat dated at a time when digital distribution has become the norm for most major-label artists and for many independent ones. When we first began research into Music 2.0 the situation was different, but now the dust is settling. In the context of this book, the term Music 2.0 helps to provide clarity about the transition between a twentieth-century model of production and distribution and the processes that are becoming standard practice in the twenty-first-century music ecology.

The impact of the new media technologies is better understood as part of a continuum of change; human engagement with music at both an individual and a social level has constantly changed throughout history, albeit marked by periods of relative stability. We argue that it is only possible to understand the future(s) of music by contextualizing post-digital events as the current point on a longer history of continuity and contestation.

Networked digital computers (and their post-PC brethren such as smartphones and tablets) have enabled an unprecedented convergence of industries and practices across all media (Meikle and Young 2012). Previously distinct media forms and their respective industries are converging and the line between production and consumption is becoming increasingly blurred as the network allows affordable and accessible distribution and publication. The global media-scape is in the midst of a noisy and hotly contested reconfiguration.

Music is a central component of this reconfiguration, and its trials and tribulations during this period have received more coverage and interest than any other media form. Arguably, because music was the first to use digital formats (with the introduction of compact discs), it was at the vanguard of the shift, and has been the canary in the coalmine for other media industries. As digital affordances have expanded, both producers and consumers of music have been newly empowered – something we explore in detail later in the book. As a consequence, the twentieth-century models of making and distributing music are under threat, as musicians and audiences embrace new (and old) opportunities, many of which bypass the incumbent beneficiaries of the pre-digital music economy.

The distinction, however, is far from clear-cut and the focus tends to be on the "music industry", largely ignoring the non-commercial production and enjoyment of music. Even there, as Williamson and Cloonan (2007: 305) point out, it is common to conflate the term "music industry" with "music recording industry". And it is also common to conflate the recording industry with the rise of popular music, and easy to forget that the present hand-wringing over the state of music is not a new phenomenon. Challenges to the status quo have consistently been attacked by those enamoured with the status quo. For example, in the early twentieth century, Theodor Adorno from the Frankfurt School was scathingly critical of popular music; while the validity of his criticism is less convincing at the dawn of the twenty-first century, his analysis of the issues arising from the commodification of music remains useful. Adorno argued that the popular music of the time was nothing more than a series of unreflective, standardized and interchangeable components – but, in aesthetic terms, Adorno's objections to popular music appear to be more clearly directed at its industrial commodification rather than the music itself. In many ways, that reaction was the natural consequence of the introduction of reproduction technologies and it is worth gesturing to Walter Benjamin's (1992: 215) observation that the introduction of mechanical reproduction resulted in our having a significantly different relationship with works of art – the aura of the original or live performance is missing in a reproduced artefact.

This also reflects the reality that commodity value depends on scarcity. Prior to mechanical reproduction, scarcity was intrinsic to the performance of music. The availability of music was limited by the number of people with sufficient talent to provide the required entertainment or services; in Marxist terms, the scarcity of labour provided the value. With the commodification of a recorded performance, that scarcity shifted to the capacity of systems of production and distribution; it was a scarcity determined by an industrial process. Today's digital technologies – with their significantly different industrial processes – have essentially destroyed those twentieth-century notions of scarcity, reducing the possibility of generating income from industrial efficiencies, and forcing many to reconsider more traditional scarcities (of labour and physical artefacts) that remain difficult to produce and distribute. In short, the industrial age of music production is being confronted by an environment that no longer includes the constraints that made possible the economic models of the industrial age.

One way of thinking about that change is with a longer view. For example, whilst it might be overly provocative to call the age of industrialization an aberration, the commodification of the recorded form could be considered a transitional phase within a much longer tradition in which the social construction of music is built around musicians and live performance. Rather than disrupting a natural order (of industrial-scale production and distribution of music) the new technologies may have actually returned us to a *more* natural order, where such commodification is less common. Indeed, the early days of the recording industry built as much on live performance as selling recorded music. And just as some contemporary musicians understand recordings as secondary to more lucrative live shows, early recording artists tended not to privilege recordings as much as late-twentieth-century industrial practices suggest. For example, in the early 1900s, Caruso's first recordings generated so much interest (and $5 million worth of sales) that the Metropolitan Opera House offered him a contract to perform there (Millard 2005: 60).

Of course, the history of the music industry is not monolithic. As well as the openly industrial approach of capital with its hit-seeking mechanisms, a large number of musicians have sought success whilst maintaining what they might term integrity or authenticity. That authenticity has been contested, with many arguing that traditional media production and distribution constrain the possibility of authenticity because the key motivation for cultural production is profit rather than art. In Bourdieu's terms, the industry – in the form of record companies, radio stations, music television and the associated marketing paraphernalia that surrounds the commodification of popular music – is made up of "cultural intermediaries", who provide symbolic goods and services. Structurally, they stand between audiences and cultural producers and present, frame and interpret all aspects of cultural production. As Fairchild (2005: 309–10) notes, "they have an agenda, one that Bourdieu saw as inherently conservative (Bourdieu 1984: 366–7). They exert a form of cultural authority as shapers of taste and values" – but they do so largely for reasons of profit.

But the recording sector represents just one facet of the music industries that include other significant areas such as live music, publishing, retail and education. Although the term "music industries" is more accurate, it is still not all-encompassing. Music is more than just industry sectors. For example, Ruth Finnegan (2007) points to the richness of amateur – and often unseen – musical activities. So whilst it might be tempting to focus solely on recorded music (see Gordon 2005; Kusek and Leonhard 2005; Leonhard 2008), it is useful to tease out the broader complexities. Just as the new technologies of a hundred years ago enabled the particular twentieth-century industrialization of music, today's new technologies are provoking possible re-industrializations – new conceptions of engaging with music that blur production and consumption, amateur and professional, performance and recording, mass and individual audiences. Combine that with the ability of all musicians to easily engage with a global network for promotion and distribution and it is clear that Music 2.0 provides opportunities for the reshaping of Bourdieu's cultural intermediaries.

In short, the bifurcated approach to discussing contemporary music (often expressed as a battle between "approved" distributors and pirates) is overly simplistic. This book endeavours to situate the Music 2.0 debate in broader terms, and to demonstrate that the particular industrialization(s) of music with which we are so familiar are part of a longer, evolving, continuum of musical engagement.

The first part of this book is concerned with technology. In contemporary common usage, the term "technology" has particular meanings that generally revolve around computing devices and digital gadgetry. But a deeper understanding of technology is key to thinking through our current media and music landscapes. Chapter 1 explores the history of music technologies, in particular the impact of radio and recording at the turn of the twentieth century. For the authors, technology has always been implicated in the evolving cultural practices around music and understanding both the role of technology and how it enables specific industrial practices provides a historical context for the current debates.

Music does not exist in isolation. It is increasingly part of a broader multimedia milieu and the changes that have occurred across the media-scape. Chapter 2 looks at the broader digital technologies and their impact and situates the Music 2.0 discussion in the context of web 2.0 and the significant changes in all other media forms, as convergence blurs previous practices and technological changes enable new opportunities for engagement.

Following on from this broader canvas, Chapter 3 focuses on current music technologies and examines the particular (digital) technologies that have reshaped music in the last decade. Once the domain of a small number of geeky experts, computer technologies have been consumerized: the powers of the microprocessor and the network have been brought to bear on the production and distribution of music. This digitization is the basis for what many are calling Music 2.0.

Although many opportunities are emerging, it is important to be aware that new relationships are also emerging – and that those new relationships are reshaping the music industry. Whilst Music 2.0 promises to allow a direct connection between artist and fan, that connection is frequently mediated by a variety of agencies, whether it be a manager, Facebook, iTunes or an online distribution aggregator. In many ways the old intermediaries are being replaced by new ones. Chapter 4 examines how the music industry is being reshaped and identifies the new players and interactions that may be occurring.

One measure of continuity is the bifurcated nature of the music industry, with a small number of "superstars" having global "hits" and other artists settling for less. Arguably, the question for the new formations is whether they include mechanisms that allow such extreme success to occur. Chapter 5 examines the examples of key artists who are bypassing the traditional approaches to music monetization. Whilst the mainstream recording industry has exhibited some reluctance to join music consumers in the digital revolution, several major artists such as David Bowie, Radiohead, Prince and Nine Inch Nails have embraced Music 2.0, grasping the opportunities with both hands. The chapter looks at some of the ways in which major artists have reconfigured their approach to distributing music and engaging their audience, displacing the recording industry and traditional contractual arrangements.

But not all artists have fan-bases of the magnitude enjoyed by Radiohead or Bowie – and many argue that their success with the new has only grown out of their success with the old. But the new media have provided many opportunities for artists to connect directly with audiences and to monetize creativity in the form of record sales, live performances and merchandise. Drawing on original research, Chapter 6 explores some of the innovations of Music 2.0 fostered at a grass-roots level, ranging from pub bands and electronic bedroom producers to artists who are achieving success in the top ten.

Historically, success in the music industry has been gauged by the number of retail units shipped and the revenue derived from sales. This will no doubt still be the case well into the future (and Music 2.0 provides new ways to exploit existing successes), but the new music environment amplifies alternative possibilities for artists. By leveraging the new technologies, artists are able to craft careers that look very different from traditional pathways. Again building on primary research, we identify examples that suggest new approaches to succeeding in the music industry, whilst acknowledging their limitations. Intriguingly, these newer approaches draw on past practices – albeit using new media technologies – which involve more direct connections between musicians and their audiences. Although such approaches may not result in the scale of reward achieved by some (relatively few) in the industrialized recording machine, it has allowed many more musicians to make a comfortable living than was previously the case. Indeed, it could be argued that Music 2.0 has seen a flattening of the music hierarchy. Whilst some would argue that there are fewer superstars, selling fewer albums and making less income, this is countered by more musicians making enough money to consider themselves professional musicians. In particular, the measures of success are themselves contested. Some musicians may countenance nothing short of a major record label deal and becoming a household name, but for others the measure of success may be generating a modest income from producing and performing the music they love.

Of course, industrial processes require state support to enshrine their production processes in law. For music (as with most other media), industrialization has relied on the protection of intellectual property and the shaping of possibility through copyright law. Chapter 7 looks at the law, particularly how copyright has shaped the music industry and how digital technologies have challenged those copyright laws. As new digital technologies threaten to make copyright enforcement a huge challenge, the emerging spectre of termination rights suggests a perfect storm for existing industry practices.

Just as history documents past struggles over music, the future of music is complex and contested. Incumbent twentieth-century institutions will struggle against change, motivated by the need to survive and profit, and emerging entities will need to engage with those particular battles for visibility and acceptance.

The new technologies have shifted the parameters of possibility; they have dramatically reconfigured time and space and redefined the boundaries within which all musicians can operate. This book aims to unpack the complexity, map the changes and explain the causes and motivations surrounding an industry and culture undergoing change.

1   The Technology of Music

Music has always been implicated with technological implementation. Whether it be the earliest incarnation of noble savages playing flutes and beating sticks together in combination with the sound of the human voice or the more recent synthesis of sounds entirely producible only by electronic means, a technological artefact has been involved. Indeed, the use of tools within the production of music allows us to assert that music *is a technology* – the production and dissemination of music is a technological system, a system whose affordances have the ability to shape not only the musical content but also the extent to which music can be produced and distributed.

On that basis, changes in technology are an integral part of the story of music. This is readily apparent from recent developments – Simon Frith (1988) argues that popular and rock music in particular only developed because of the enabling technologies of the twentieth century. But even before pop and rock, human engagement with music was shaped by musical instruments and the expressive possibilities of the tools that we have used to create music. Initially, the technology of music was limited to the technology of instrumentation. Beyond the human voice, innovation rose with the development of wind, string and percussion instruments that enabled a range of sounds and timbres to be played by individual musicians. The wooden bodies of stringed instruments and the metal bells of brass instruments allowed humans to play more loudly, to project further and to perform with a greater range of dynamics, nuances which were further enhanced by the creation of musical ensembles such as orchestras. The establishment of concert halls co-opted architecture into the technology of musical performance, enabling large groups of people to enjoy the same musical performance.

Electrical machines followed. Acoustic amplification was supplemented by electrical devices, allowing a more affordable solution for playing to big audiences; the subtle acoustics of a specially designed theatre were no longer necessary for such activities. Broadcast technologies expanded those audiences in a completely different direction and the introduction of recording tools displaced the need for performance entirely, reconfiguring how music was created and disseminated.

Prior to broadcasting and recording, the only way to enjoy music in a domestic situation was to play it yourself or listen to someone who could play music – either their own compositions or from published sheet music. J. Michael Keyes (2004: 410) notes that in the early 1800s the piano was responsible for providing the majority of domestic entertainment in American households. In that pre-recording era the music industry consisted primarily of sheet-music publishers and was more comparable to the book publishing trade than its contemporary incarnation. By 1887 the piano's popularity was entrenched, with some 500,000 American children learning to play (Parlor Songs Academy). The increasing popularity of the piano saw a concomitant demand for sheet music, leading to the rise of "Tin Pan Alley" – a collection of sheet-music publishers in the neighbourhood of 28th Street, Manhattan – and a more industrialized approach to music. The publishers of Tin Pan Alley hired songwriters (including George Gershwin and Cole Porter) and sold the products of their artistic labours as sheet music. Towards the end of the nineteenth century publishers realized an alternative revenue opportunity in live performances of the works they had commissioned. In the United States this resulted in an 1897 copyright law amendment granting an exclusive right in the public performance of music for profit and the eventual establishment of the American Society of Composers, Authors and Publishers (ASCAP). This exclusive right and similar societies had been established in a number of European countries in the second half of the nineteenth century. As Keyes (2004: 414) points out, through copyright law the music publishers of Tin Pan Alley "had control over the two main modes by which the public consumed music" – the production of sheet music and its public performance.

The introduction of recording technologies toward the end of the nineteenth century irrevocably altered the musical landscape. Apart from the obvious initial performance, recordings meant that a live musician was no longer required to play music – enjoying music was suddenly much more accessible. As well, the recording systems themselves developed and allowed more sophisticated layering of instrumentation and new musical compositions to occur.

"Recording" conjures up images of vinyl records, cassette tapes and compact discs, but an early (and successful) venture into recording sound was the development of mechanical pianos. Edward Votey produced the Pianola in 1895 and with the backing of the Aeolin Corporation it went into mass production two years later. The Pianola was a piano designed to be self-playing. A pianist's performance was captured on a piano specially designed to record it by making perforations in paper rolls to indicate the pitch and duration of notes. Additional control data could be entered in a side column of the roll to produce dynamics such as pedal use and attack times. These paper rolls were inserted into the Pianola, which then mechanically scrolled through the perforations, translating them into a performance of actual hammer and pedal actions on the instrument. The development of mechanical pianos prompted an amendment to U.S. copyright law. In 1897 Adam Geibel composed 'Little Cotton Baby' and 'Kentucky Babe' and assigned his copyrights in the songs to the White-Smith Music Company, his sheet-music publisher. The Apollo Company began producing piano rolls of Geibel's songs without paying any royalties to White-Smith, leading the latter to initiate a lawsuit for copyright infringement. The Supreme Court heard the case in 1908. The law of the time prohibited copying of sheet music but made no mention of performances. The court found no infringement, drawing a distinction between sheet music and piano rolls: "These perforated rolls are parts of a machine which, when duly applied and properly operated in connection with the mechanism to which they are adapted, produce musical tones in harmonious combination. But we cannot think that they are copies within the meaning of the copyright act" (*White-Smith Music Pub. Co.* v. *Apollo Co.* 209 US. 1,18 [1908]). This decision allowed piano-roll manufacturers (and early phonograph companies) to record and distribute music without paying the original composer or publisher any royalties. The ruling was superseded the following year, when the Copyright Act 1909 introduced a statutory compulsory licence, thus enabling musical works to flourish in the new technological environment while ensuring that copyright owners would receive royalties for performances.

The Pianola and its subsequent competitors are the ancestors of modern MIDI sequencers such as Cubase which still utilize the metaphor of the "piano roll" to describe one of the means for inputting note and controller information. As well as removing the need for a physical musician, the mechanical piano transcended human limitations; a score could be constructed of such complexity that no pianist could physically play it – to that extent, mechanical piano systems anticipated the multitrack recording that would emerge in later years.

Moving away from live performance, the invention of the phonograph and radio reconfigured our relationships with music and set the stage for a new trajectory for the music industries. As Frith notes (1988: 19–22), the rise of popular music happened in partnership with the introduction of the vinyl record, the development of broadcast radio systems and then the coming of the CD, the first of the mainstream digital technologies.

Importantly, each of the technologies mentioned was the catalyst for new social relationships. As business models emerged out of exploiting the new techniques of reproduction and dissemination, industries evolved – and (just as copyright law expanded under pressure from music publishers in the Pianola example) the social and legal frameworks for the business of music were shaped by their underpinning technologies. The example of radio, whose possibilities of two-way communication were constrained in the early 1900s by a combination of legal and technical restriction, is illustrative. Whilst recorded music was not a factor in the early development of radio, broadcasting would be instrumental in expanding its popularity – the affordances of the broadcast model would shape the popular music industry for most of the twentieth century.

As with any technological system, the relationships between the actors involved are antagonistic. In the music ecology interactions and competing motivations between performers, audiences, intermediaries, instrumentation, performance and recording technologies are played out within the constraints allowed by technological possibility. As technologies evolve, the dimensions of that contest also shift and what might have appeared to be a settled state can be clearly seen as another temporary step in an ongoing evolutionary struggle. A consequence of this struggle is that the boundaries between particular roles can blur; for example, the line between musician and audience or performer and publisher can shift. What some might argue is the natural order of things might be better understood as a relatively short period of stability in a longer history of continually shifting relationships. In that context, the current upheavals in the music industry are merely the latest development in a continuum of change.

Understanding Technology

It is tempting (particularly in the current environment) to cast technological change as the driver of these shifting relationships, but the reality is that technology itself seldom *determines* outcomes. Instead, changes in technologies provide opportunities that allow social and cultural practices to change – without new music technologies change is unlikely, but technological changes are a condition, rather than a driver, of change. While it is not the core aim of this book to delve into the relationships between technology and society, an understanding of those relationships provides a useful framework for thinking about Music 2.0.

The most simplistic (and arguably most common) way of thinking about technology is a deterministic one. In this approach, technology is seen as the driver of social change: the introduction of a new machine wreaks predictable havoc on the social and cultural life on which it is unleashed. In this view, technology is conceived as a locomotive on a train track, carving a predestined, inevitable path to the future. Or, in the music context, the introduction of radio results in the recording industry as we know it. Such deterministic approaches are common – whether dystopian or utopian, the inevitable shaping of social behaviour by some wondrous (or dangerous) new technology is a recurring theme.

In *Understanding Media*, Marshall McLuhan argued that technologies are "extensions of man" and that technological change causes a fundamental shift in the nature of those extensions (1964: 8). For McLuhan, the introduction of electricity was illustrative; whereas the preceding mechanical age primarily harnessed mechanical power to extend the physical capabilities of human bodies, the electric age witnessed the extension of human senses by information and communication media, technologies such as the telephone, radio and television. Whereas mechanical technologies extended our limbs, electric technologies extended our nervous system. Central to his account is the argument that the technologies we use shape, if not *determine*, our worlds. More explicitly in the media realm, McLuhan argued that the type of media used was more important than the content it carries, that dominant communication technologies determine possibilities and consequently what can be thought and said. Thus television would provoke a different response to a newspaper, even if they were ostensibly communicating the same content. Some argue that the Kennedy–Nixon presidential debates of 1960 offer some support to McLuhan's argument (Sparks 2010: 293). The reactions of the public differed greatly depending on whether the debate was watched on television or listened to on the radio.

However, pure technological determinism is an inadequate approach that ignores or downplays the numerous other factors that surround the implementation of new technologies and their social impact. For example, Langdon Winner distinguishes between determinism and conditioning (Winner 1978: 192–210). Determinism grants agency to the technology, suggesting that it gives people *no choice* in how they might live. Similarly, Paul Levinson argues for a distinction between what he calls soft and hard determinism. He suggests that if a technology has an inevitable, irresistible social effect, then a hard determinism exists, and he cites the example of the relationship between an abstract language and humanity. However, he acknowledges that technologies almost inevitably have unintended consequences, and most technologies should be understood as having the capacity to "make events possible – events whose shape and impact are the result of factors other than the [information] technology at hand" (1997: 3). Levinson refers to such determinisms as "soft". In other words, technologies create certain *possibilities* for interpretative flexibility, but do not necessarily determine the outcome.

In the case of radio, its eventual use as a mass medium – broadcasting Bing Crosby to the world – was a somewhat different implementation of its technologies, which had initially been used by amateurs and professionals alike as two-way communication tools. Similarly, the turntable manufacturers of the 1960s and 1970s would never have expected a passive playback device to be subverted into an active instrument by Afrika Bambaataa or Grandmaster Flash. More recently, the Fraunhofer-Gesellschaft did not predict that its research into low-bit-rate, high-quality audio compression would result in the digital format *du jour* that would be the springboard for so much turmoil in the recording industry and so much opportunity for artists. As science-fiction author William Gibson famously noted, "the street finds its own uses for things – uses the manufacturers never imagined" (1989: 85).

In contrast to technological determinism, the relative importance of social factors (as distinct from technical ones) in technological developments is seen in ideas such as the Social Construction of Technology (SCOT). SCOT emerged as a counterpoint to technological determinism and situated technologies clearly in a dynamic system that involves humans as well as machines. Pinch and Bijker (1987: 28–46) initially articulated SCOT, using the development of the safety bicycle as an example. They argue that the safety bicycle emerged over a number of years in the late nineteenth century and involved a number of human interventions, as well as technical developments. In that particular case, the bicycle evolved due to factors that included the desire by women to become bicycle riders and the invention of the pneumatic tyre. Actor Network Theory (ANT) develops SCOT (Callon and Latour 1981) to describe a network of technological systems populated by "actants" – an extension of the notion of an actor beyond that of a human player, allowing for non-human participants such as texts or machines. For example, driving a car involves a number of factors – the road rules, one's driving experience and the physical capabilities of the car are all connected. ANT suggests that the act of driving should be considered together with all of its linked influencing factors.

The role of governments can be enormous. In particular, the priorities of war can cause states to privilege certain technological implementations whilst limiting others. The outbreak of World War I led the US Navy to claim the airwaves, shutting down amateur radio broadcasts and communication, reshaping the possibilities of radio and de-emphasizing its amateur actants. A complementary reading (Hargittai 2000: 52) suggests the sinking of the *Titanic* as a possible turning point for how radio could be used. Its previous utilization as a communications tool for enthusiasts was challenged when there was a suggestion that the *Titanic* rescue effort was hampered by confusion in the airwaves. The result was more stringent regulation of the broadcast frequencies. Combined with the US Navy's claim to control the airwaves, a more heavily regulated radio sector paved the way for its corporatization.

The interesting point to be derived from these discussions is that there is often an "idea" which informs the implementation of a technology and extends beyond the technology itself. Whereas a technological determinist approach would understand a technology to be true only unto itself, the presence of social ideas external to the technology allows for a more useful analytical framework and diminishes the autonomy found in technological determinist arguments. Whilst technologists would undoubtedly argue that their creations incorporate an idea (the solution to a technical problem, even an acknowledgement of business imperatives), the notion that distinctive abstractions can be imposed onto a technology is an important one because it suggests that a technology may be designed (or selected) for an overtly political or commercial reason, embracing a particular social concept as its *raison d'être*. For example, Mark Zuckerberg's social network leviathan Facebook was reportedly founded on high-minded ideals: "If people share more, the world will become more open and connected. And a world that's more open and connected is a better world" (Kakutani 2010). Facebook's struggles for profitability despite its enormous user base hint at the tensions between its cultural beginnings and its fiscal responsibilities to shareholders.

In short, a technological system is as much an idea (in a wider social and political sense) as it is an engineering solution. Taking such an approach makes it possible to consider the competing ideologies and desires that inform a stable form of a particular technological possibility, and by pursuing it or (in Latour's words) "following the actors" we can understand not only the past and present, but also the possible futures of technological implementations.

And so it is with music technologies.

The Musical Experience

The experience of music has always been a constructed one: an assemblage of ideas, actors and technologies in often-contested combinations that achieve a period of stability before moving through the next contested period. Moreover, there are multiple constructions of music – many ways in which the musical experience is built involving a variety of actors in different cultural settings. A number of dichotomies can be identified. The musical experience can be private or public; personal or communal; performer or audience; commodified or otherwise. What is clear is that technological implementations have different affordances that encourage various combinations of those features. The twentieth-century model, for example, encouraged the commodification of recorded performance for private audiences, often by marketing the aura of public, communal live performances. More recent developments saw the audience become producer (with the advent of accessible remix opportunities) and the private blend with the public at "headphone party" nights, where all clubbers share the same music experience through the intimacy of headphones.

What we have come to know as the music industry is a particular combination of practices and possibilities. Whilst we may consider the current state of play as natural, music has been experienced in many different ways throughout history, leading to a confluence of contemporary activities. The practice of music has always been enjoyed by individuals, families and other non-commercial groups as an integral part of community life and values. Although often codified in hymn books and folk songs, music was not always commodified; commercial gain from shared practice is a recent innovation of the music industries. Music is multidimensional – its capacity for commodification represents just one facet of its intrinsic value. In *Music in Everyday Life*, Tia DeNora identifies music as a technology of self and reveals some aspects of our personal relationships with music (2000: 46–74). One of DeNora's interviewees leads her to the conclusion that "music has transformative powers, it 'does' things, changes things, makes things happen". She continues on to discuss the aesthetic reflexivity that occurs when individuals use music almost as a form of self-medication – to create, accentuate or break moods. Philip Bohlman rethinks various ontologies of music and questions the veracity of our assumptions about it. For example, he draws attention to the connections between music, memory and time as well as critiquing assumptions that music is inherently beautiful (2001: 30–1). Bohlman contends that "thinking music" privileges a particular approach to the exclusion of others, whereas "rethinking music" positively lacks "conviction that any ontological process is ultimately knowable; we rethink music out of the belief that we missed something the first time round" (2001: 34). As Keyes (2004. 421) summarizes, "There is no question that music speaks to us in mysterious and profound ways and invokes within us numerous physiological and emotional responses"; it is useful to be reminded that the value of music is not merely pecuniary. Our relationships with music are usually emotionally charged and complex and the idea of profiting from music is not an essential component of everyone's musical experience.

The adoption – and indeed adaptation – of recording and communications technologies illustrates the tensions. Given the primacy of music in the human experience, engaging with music, and sharing those musical engagements, motivates many musicians. So it is no surprise that technologies are used for what may be categorized as multiple purposes and the recent history of music technologies is informative.

For example, the printing press did much to promulgate the commodification and commercialization of literature, and its mechanisms were put to the same purpose for music. Of course, the distribution of sheet music was a means to enable widespread performance. The publication of sheet music created an artefact that allowed the repeated *production* of performance (rather than a *reproduction* of a single performance – this would come later with recording technologies) and benefited generations of professional musicians. Arguably, it was demand from musicians to have the ability to recreate a musical experience that drove the widespread adoption of sheet music. Of course, that artefact could be bought and sold. Ownership of sheet-music rights led music publishers to realize that public performance could present an additional and lucrative source of revenue – and the industrialization of music was enabled. Publishers sold sheet music *and* licensed the right to perform that music commercially. Although music was still enjoyed personally and socially, the period between the late nineteenth century and the early twentieth century saw it take on an additional and new form of value.

Although the seeds for the industrialization of music were planted with the emergence of the nineteenth century's sheet-music and performance economies, the twentieth century marked a particular and more familiar incarnation of music – a key shift toward the industrialization of a recorded artefact. Frith distinguishes this characterization of twentieth-century music from earlier incarnations:

> The industrialization of music cannot be understood as something which happens to music, since it describes a process in which music itself is made – a process, that is, which fuses (and confuses) capital, technical and musical arguments. Twentieth-century popular music means the twentieth-century popular record; not the record of something (a song? a singer? a performance?) which exists independently of the music industry, but a form of communication which determines what songs, singers and performances are and can be. (2006: 231)

He sees the shift towards the recorded artefact as the primary mode for enjoyment of music as being fuelled by three key elements: the development of recording technologies; the economy of making money from music; and finally the establishment of what he refers to as a "new musical culture" that reshaped how music was discovered, produced and consumed (2006: 232).

Frith details the history of industrialization and argues that

> [by] 1945 the basic structure of the modern music industry was in place. Pop music meant pop records, commodities, a technological and commercial process under the control of a small number of

> large companies. Such control depended on the ownership of the means of record production and distribution, and was organized around the marketing of stars and star performances (just as the music publishing business had been organized around the manufacture and distribution of songs). Live music making was still important but its organization and profits were increasingly dependent on the exigencies of record making. The most important way of publicizing pop – the way most people heard most music – was on the radio, and records were made with radio formats and radio audiences in mind. (Frith 2006: 236)

This represented a shift from music as performance and publishing to music as recorded artefact, and the industry's focus for much of the twentieth century was on commodifying and exploiting that recorded artefact.

As alluded to earlier, the development of radio provides a key example in the adoption of music technologies. After World War I, radio's potential for broadcasting music emerged. Frank Conrad, a Westinghouse Corporation engineer working on radio technology for the war effort, made a test broadcast using a phonograph. Unbeknownst to him, he had an audience of illegal listeners defying government orders to clear the airwaves. Conrad continued to broadcast to his audience every Saturday night. After the wartime ban ended in 1918, he resumed his amateur broadcasts, playing music to his audience from his own record collection. Realizing the limits of his collection, Conrad struck a deal to play on air records supplied by his local record store in return for promoting the store during his broadcast. Conrad was arguably the first radio DJ and pioneer for radio commercials; his popularity grew through the early 1920s and a store in his native Pittsburgh started selling radio sets so people could receive his transmissions. A vice-president at Westinghouse saw an advertisement for a radio capable of receiving Conrad's broadcasts and realized the potential for mass communication. The popularity of radio inspired Westinghouse to apply for an official broadcasting licence and KDKA Radio was born just in time for the US presidential election on 2 November 1920 (Wood 1992: 13).

In what might be cast as a parallel to current debates over uses of internet technologies, the shift from amateur sharing of material to institutionalized control of radio broadcasting paved the way for its commodification and informed the shaping of the twentieth-century music industry.

In the first two decades of the twentieth century record companies were intimately connected with the playback technologies employed to listen to music and were little more than a specialized part of the electric goods industry:

> They were owned and run by engineers, inventors and stock market speculators. They had little to do with song publishers, theatre owners, agents, promoters or performers. Their managers did not seem much interested in music.(Frith 2007: 98)

The industry was firmly focused on the sale of records, not necessarily the sale of music. The sale of recorded music still remains the dominant focus of record labels, and whilst it may seem that little has changed in the last hundred years, the twenty-first century is an era characterized by significant challenges to that model.

That twentieth-century model for the music industries remains a response to the affordances of the particular technologies across the dimensions of time and space. As newer technologies developed, the constraints of space, time and cost were redefined, resulting in new possibilities for musical engagement. Continuing advancements in recording technologies mean that nowadays any musician (or anyone so inclined) can record for a minimal budget. Increased power in desktop and laptop computing technologies and affordable or sometimes free software provide access to multitrack software, virtual synthesizers, samplers and effects. Damon Albarn even recorded Gorillaz's fourth album, *The Fall* (2010), on an early iPad. Recording technology that was once reserved for large corporations is now available to many. And although selling as many recordings as possible may drive record labels, not everyone in the new music economy is similarly motivated. The remainder of this chapter explores that development of recording technologies. We identify how the impact of technological change across specific dimensions has shifted our musical experience. For the present authors, how recording technologies have allowed the reshaping of space and time is key to understanding how the music industries are being reshaped.

Recording: Confronting Space and Time

Communications technologies have always changed the availability of information across space and time, with a subsequent impact on our social relationship with that information. The printing press, the telegraph and the radio all constructed particular spatial and temporal opportunities and their technological development provoked further change. In the realm of music, before recording there was only performance, an activity that required audience and performer to occupy the same space at the same time. Whether in private spaces gathered around the family piano, public performances at the theatre or the in-between space of recitals for invited guests, the experience of music demanded the bringing together of musician(s) and audience into the same physical and temporal space. One of the key affordances of recording is spatial and temporal dissociation of performer and audience. The introduction of recording technologies removed the immediacy of performance from music consumption, time-shifting it – bending playback to the whim of the listener. Individual audience members can share a recorded experience regardless of their arbitrary positions in space and time. And not only does space shift locally, but recording technologies create a diasporic audience connected by an experience of the same event regardless of geographical and temporal distance. The development of distribution mechanisms for those recordings as either objects or performance themselves (via radio) enabled the emergence of what became the "majors" of the contemporary music industry. During the twentieth century, music for many became synonymous with recorded music – and the industry's growth reflected that reality.

Some of the first recordings ever made were the product of Édouard-Léon Scott de Martinville's phonautograph, an attempt to create the audio equivalent of the camera. It was a purely mechanical device that used a stylus to record sound waves onto paper blackened by oil-lamp smoke. But the phonautograph was fundamentally flawed by its inability to play back its own recordings. Instead de Martinville envisioned that people would actually be able to read the recorded patterns visually (Van Buskirk 2010), requiring a new form of musical literacy. It took nearly 150 years for these early recordings to be heard by human ears. In 2008 the American audio history group First Sounds managed to play back a 10-second rendition of the French folk song 'Au clair de la lune, Pierrot répondit', recorded by de Martinville in 1860. If any single instance exemplifies the extension of time and space afforded by recording technologies, then this is it.

Although de Martinville's phonautograph predates Thomas Edison's foray into recording, it is Edison who is popularly associated with pioneering such technologies. He conceived the phonograph in 1877 while attempting to record telegraph transmissions and to automate telephonic messages. Edison's media of choice were cylinders wrapped in metal foil, but his early patents indicate that he had considered recording onto a disc, the shape that was eventually adopted for vinyl, mini-disc and CD. Within a matter of years the phonograph's capabilities had been applied to music. One of the oldest surviving phonograph cylinders is a recording of Handel's choral music as performed in 1888. A demonstration recording from 1906 proclaims the phonograph's usefulness for delivering music:

> I am the Edison phonograph, created by the great wizard of the New World to delight those who would have melody or be amused. I can sing you tender songs of love. I can give you merry tales and joyous laughter. I can transport you to the realms of music. I can

cause you to join in the rhythmic dance. I can lull the babe to sweet
repose, or waken in the aged heart soft memories of youthful days.
No matter what may be your mood, I am always ready to enter-
tain you. When your day's work is done, I can bring the theater or
the opera to your home. I can give you grand opera, comic opera or
vaudeville. I can give you sacred or popular music, dance, orchestra
or instrumental music. I can render solos, duets, trios, quartets. (A
copy of this recording in OGG format is available courtesy of Wikipedia – http://en.wikipedia.org/wiki/File:Advertising_Record.ogg)

As the transcription above suggests, music could now be enjoyed domestically without having to go out to the theatre or dance hall. Arguably, Edison's
phonograph represented the first steps in commercial and industrial reproduction of music, but it was not long before other players entered the market.
Volta Associates preferred to market wax discs engraved with grooves rather
than adopt Edison's use of cylinders and although the two formats coexisted
for some time between 1895 and 1920, the familiar shape of the disc eventually supplanted cylinders.

In 1914, when the patents in manufacturing discs expired, the market
opened for competition and discs became the dominant format. In 1916 there
were 46 phonograph companies in existence, with sales between 1914 and
1919 soaring from $27 million to over $158 million (Frith 1988: 14). By the
1920s, phonograph (also known as gramophone) records were the format
of choice. The cylinder had all but been replaced, the victim of a format war
just as Betamax would fall to VHS decades later. Ironically, Edison – the archi-
tect of sound recordings – dropped out of the recording business in 1929 for
two key reasons. First, his dislike of the genre prevented him from capitalizing on the burgeoning market for jazz records. Second, his late adoption of
the disc format prejudiced his market position. The Edison Disc was produced
between 1912 and 1929 but by then the Victor Talking Machine Company
and the Columbia Phonograph Company had established a dominant market
share (Wikström 2009: 62–3). This period marked the start of the recording
industry, with Edison Recording, the Victor Talking Machine Company and the
Columbia Phonograph Company as its "Big Three". An industrialized process
of music production had taken shape.

The process of recording allowed music to be enjoyed without the immediate presence of a performance for the first time in history. These opportunities were furthered by the development of radio broadcasting technologies.
At the time radio provided a perfect medium for distributing music, allowing it to be diffused via the airwaves to groups of people or individuals. The
broadcast radio industry and the recorded music industry developed hand in
hand; for much of the twentieth century, the primary way for popular musi-

cians to get exposure was through radio airplay. The relationship between radio and the music industries has been a privileged one, especially in the USA, where traditional broadcast radio stations (as opposed to digital audio transmissions) are exempt from having to pay to play sound recordings on the air. Songwriters and holders of the publishing copyright still receive royalties, but recording artists do not. Edward Fritts, representing the National Association of Broadcasters, pointed out that (in the American tradition)

> [the] history of copyright protection for sound recordings reflects a dominant, recurring theme: Congress repeatedly took pains to ensure that the grant of copyright protection did not affect the symbiotic relationship between the radio broadcasters and the record industry. Congress recognized both that the record industry reaps huge benefits from the public performance of their recordings by radio stations, and that the granting of a public performance right could alter that relationship to the detriment of both industries. (US Congress, House. Committee on the Judiciary, 15 June 2000)

This special and symbiotic relationship between the two industries has, however, sometimes skirted along the edge of ethically acceptable behaviour. There is a history of record companies providing financial incentives for radio stations to promote certain records ahead of others. Radio play was considered so important to the success of a record (and therefore profits) that the major labels were prepared to buy airplay for selected releases. In the mid-twentieth century, this pay-for-play scheme was known as "payola" – a word that was conferred on the English language by the recording industry. Two of the individuals to feature most prominently in the first payola scandal were DJs Alan Freed and Dick Clark. In 1960 the District Attorney for New York investigated both men for accepting bribes in exchange for playing specific songs on their respective radio and TV programmes. Clark (who was not charged) was the more fortunate of the two; Freed was charged with receiving bribes totalling $2500. His situation was worsened by the fact that he claimed co-writing credits on several songs and profited every time he played them on his radio show. Although he received just a small fine, his career declined until his death in 1965. Payola itself was not actually illegal in New York at that time and Freed was charged under commercial bribery laws. Legislation designed specifically to combat payola was subsequently passed but was obviously ineffective, as by 1990 there had not been a single prosecution (Dannen 1990: 45).

The contemporary counterpart of payola is independent promotion. Unlike payola, independent promotion is legal provided that certain conditions are met. Arguably, independent promotion is the driving force behind selections for Top 40 radio playlists. The costs involved in independent promotion are

considerable and make access to radio the province of the economically dominant major recording labels. The anti-payola statute failed to prevent the for-
mation of "The Network" during the late 1980s. "The Network" was a "loose
alliance of promoters … who exerted considerable influence over the records
played" (Dannen 1990: 11).

Independent record promoters rarely act in the interests of small labels or
music that is not accommodated by radio-station format. It is a costly and currently necessary evil for promoting a record on the airwaves and it can cost
a record label between $1000 and $8000 to have one record added to a Top
40 or rock station. On average, just twelve weeks are afforded to a record to
achieve success (which means recouping all expenses and generating a sales
profit) before the next wave of releases. With a twelve-week window in which
to ensure that a record makes a profit, promotion is paramount. Only the
major labels have sufficient finance capital to invest in a promotional consideration regime. Minor labels and more alternative or fringe artists are unable
to accommodate the costs involved in servicing the promotional scheme.
This results in the charts representing what Street (1986: 116) terms "highly
selective populism" and the marginalization of minor artists "into particular
regions or specific formats where they reach a limited audience".

Dirk Lance, bass player for Incubus, complains, "Independent promotion is
money that disappears from a band's pocket, that is charged to the band, and
no one knows where it goes or what it actually does" (Boehlert 2002). Independent promotion is a complex and significant consideration when examining how the major recording labels promote their artists. Commentators
estimate that independent promotion costs the record industry $100 to $150
million per year (Boehlert 2001).

The reconfiguration of time and space that emerged as a consequence of
recording and broadcast technologies and their concomitant industries saw
a radical shift in the construction of music. The emphasis moved away from
experiencing music in real time to music as an artefact – the recorded media
form. The new industrialized format reshaped the consumption of music,
offering a more socially ubiquitous media form that could now be experienced outside the domains of theatre halls and the domestic parlour. Additionally, the new emphasis on the recorded artefact provided the impetus for
the growth of a music industry built on its production, distribution and marketing across a range of complementary mechanisms.

Duplication: Conquering Space and Time

Although the application of Edison's phonograph to music gave birth to
a recording industry, the industrialization of music was not complete until

copies of sufficient quality could be manufactured *en masse*. The capacity to duplicate recordings pushed the trajectory of music further away from performance towards a commodified artefact. The performance was a unique and transient event whereas the recorded artefact was fixed, ready to be played back forever.

Duplication of analogue media was a laborious process involving making multiple copies of a master recording, or essentially *recordings of a recording*. Before 1890, a recording was as unique as the performance it captured, but during that decade Edison employed a pantograph mechanism to duplicate phonograph cylinders. This method, however, had significant limitations. Pantographic reproduction was limited to around 25 copies of significantly lower quality than the original. Additionally, the pantographic duplication method destroyed the original recording. At that time there was no way to produce multiple copies of a single recording at an industrial level. As Gronow and Saunio recount, "Ten phonographs would be placed in front of a loud-voiced singer or a small brass band, and in this way ten recordings would be made of one performance" (1998: 3). This approach allowed subsequent pantographic duplication to yield saleable copies numbering in the hundreds. If the market demanded more recordings, then the performance would have to be repeated. It took until 1908 to devise a moulding process for the cylinder format, which also increased the audio quality of copies. Early improvements on Edison's recording technology coincided with the commercial desire to mass produce recorded music. Emile Berliner patented the gramophone in 1888. Its basic operation mirrored that of Edison's phonograph, but it used flat discs on which the needle vibrated from side to side in engraved grooves rather than the vertical motion employed by Edison's device. More importantly, Berliner fully intended to produce recorded music industrially and to surpass Edison's existing limitations on duplication. Berliner's duplication process was ready in the 1890s and, although the audio quality was poorer than from Edison's cylinders, gramophone records could be manufactured much more quickly. Company annual reports for 1897/1898 indicate some 408,195 gramophone records had been produced.

For as long as gramophone records dominated the market, duplication was a cumbersome and expensive process, so this market was left relatively untouched by unauthorized reproduction. When recording technologies developed further and new media forms entered the fray the possibilities for duplication became more affordable and accessible (both at the industrial level and in the private sphere). Although this chapter is not concerned with "piracy", the read/write nature of later recording technologies should be noted. Edison's early phonographs were capable of recording but this feature was eventually discarded from later players. It was not until magnetic tape arrived that record-ing and duplication could easily occur outside of the industrial process.

The rise of magnetic tape is well documented in Daniel, Mee and Clark's *Magnetic Recording: The First 100 Years* (1999). Magnetic tape emerged in the late 1920s when Fritz Pfleumer built on Vlademar Poulson's earlier magnetic wire and coated a long strip of paper with iron oxide. It was a closely held state secret until the Allies extracted the technology during the final years of World War II. Tape technology was subsequently developed further and sold to American markets. In the 1950s music aficionados used reel-to-reel tape recorders – the precursors of cassette players. Compared to the production of vinyl records, tape was much more affordable and reintroduced a writable recording technology into the private sphere. Philips unveiled the compact cassette at the Berlin Radio Show in 1963 and mass production of audiocas-settes followed in 1965. Because it offered fairly limited recording fidelity, the compact cassette was initially marketed as a business tool for voice dicta-tion. But tape formulations improved, and technologies such as Dolby noise reduction (introduced in the early 1970s) made it suitable for music record-ing. Through the 1970s, compact cassettes became a mainstream distribution mechanism, a more compact and portable alternative to vinyl records that enabled the introduction of portable music players such as the Sony Walk-man, which drove the uptake of music by young people in particular. The first wave of Walkman sales was primarily to music fans in their mid-twenties, but the later mass uptake was largely due its fashionable status as a new way for teenagers to consume music (Nathan 1999: 154).

The commercial recording industry was not the only beneficiary of the compact cassette; the ease of dubbing (using double-cassette decks) led to home copying and mass duplication by organized pirates. But others also used the technology – amateur musicians looking to distribute their music could employ the same technologies as were used to pirate pre-recorded audiocas-settes. Independent cassette distribution was far from elegant. It required an initial outlay on blank cassettes and a laborious effort in creating (not to men-tion folding) inlays and application of labels, but small-scale distribution was possible. In an interview with Ian Peddie, Pacific Northwest recording artist Cory Brewer explained how his parents' stereo equipment drove a cassette-based label:

> Almost all the stuff that I put out ... was just recorded on the hand-held, low-fi tape recorder ... [copies were made] on my parents' tape desk; I would just sit for hours on end and I would just put it on high speed dubbing and watch television while I was doing it. (Peddie 2006: 166)

Robin James's edited collection *Cassette Mythos* (1990) similarly documents many artists' use of cassette tape to self-market. Although mainstream distribution through the big high-street bricks-and-mortar retailers was out of reach, cassettes represented an unprecedented freedom. Peter Manuel (1993: xiv) characterized audiocassettes as "micro-media" allowing "decentralization, democratization and dispersal", potential channels for music expression without being filtered through the mainstream industry that might be regarded as elitist. In some ways the democratic accessibility to cassette foretold the MP3 format's ability to bypass the mainstream gatekeepers of music. This is perhaps best emphasized by bands such as the Grateful Dead and Phish which – in addition to releasing albums through major labels and their subsidiaries – capitalized on cassette trading of live performances to build their respective fan bases.

The micro-media approach to independent music distribution grew further with the introduction of compact discs (CDs). Although introduced initially as a read-only technology, by the late 1990s CD writers became commonplace in home PCs, allowing easy digital reproduction. Combined with multitrack software such as Cubase, independent musicians could easily produce their own music on home-burned CDs. Building on a tradition of micro-media that had started with cassettes, such CDs offered high audio quality and a far less volatile physical medium. As with cassettes, CDs could be used as promotional material. The Arctic Monkeys recount how "we used to record demos and then just burn them onto CDs and give them away at gigs" (Park 2005). Although the qualitative benefits of CDs far outweighed those of cassettes, the duplication process was still slow and cumbersome for those operating outside the industrialized process. Unlike cassettes, however, the music on CDs could be easily ripped from the physical vessel to be stored in any number of digital audio formats on a computer for playback, although MP3 became the preferred choice of the masses. The Arctic Monkeys refer to the labour-intensive (non-industrial) CD production process: "Obviously there weren't many demos available, so people used to share them on the internet, which was a good way for everyone to hear it" (Park 2005).

Cassette tapes offered independent musicians duplication, but not to the industrialized level used by the recording industry, and the process was fraught with technological limitations and low quality. CDs improved upon cassettes with increased and also non-degradable quality. The promises and freedoms of both media stumbled over distribution. Without access to the distribution networks and retail outlets prized by the mainstream recording industry, independent musicians had few opportunities to reach large audiences. The subsequent MP3 format radically changed this. (MP3 is discussed in more detail later.)

The attraction of purely digital music lies in its ability to be duplicated flaw-lessly. When Michael Robertson and Greg Flores founded the (original) mp3.com in 1997 they offered musicians a means of distributing their music to potential audiences of thousands. To achieve this reach with cassette or CD would have required hours of painstaking manual duplication unless one could afford the processes of a commercial duplication system. But even when thousands of units were produced, then what? Independent artists were hard pushed, if not completely obstructed from getting their music into a high-street record store or played on a major radio station. Perhaps the local second-hand record store would sell them, and a few might be sold or given away at gigs. Possibly that mate who knows someone who runs a pirate radio station might be able to negotiate some airtime. In contrast, MP3 files could be distrib-uted to thousands of individuals simply by uploading one copy to a distribution service, whether this was a peer-to-peer service, a blog or a website.

The popularity of the MP3 format began to rise during the latter half of the 1990s through playback software such as Nullsoft's Winamp (released in 1997) and hardware players like Diamond's Rio PMP300. The appeal of MP3 was further encouraged by peer-to-peer services such as Napster and websites like mp3.com that offered thousands of free mp3s by independent musicians. We examine the rise of online digital distribution more fully in a later chapter, but it is important to locate MP3's position in the tradition of micro-media.

Layering – Reclaiming Lost Time

Another key reconfiguration of time through recording is layering or multi-tracking. Up until this point, we have explored how the recorded artefact was the focus of a new music economy. Layering looks to the construction of recorded music as an artefact itself.

Early recordings were monophonic (recorded on one channel), but stereo-phonic sound emerged when Alan Blumlein joined Columbia in 1929 and patented stereo (or in his own words, "binaural") sound in 1931 (Martland 1997: 137). At the time Blumlein was employed by the Columbia Grapho-phone Company (which through a merger with the Gramophone Company became EMI in 1931), where he had also significantly improved on the audio quality produced by Bell Labs' disc-cutting technique. The left-right balance of the two channels was set at the time of recording and could not be altered after the fact. The rigidity of the process echoed de Martinville's earlier aim to create a device that captured sound in the same way that the camera captured light. For a large portion of its history, recording technology was exactly that, only capable of recording the immediate performance.

Experiments with overdubbing and multitrack recordings radically changed not only how music was recorded but also how recordings were perceived. Suddenly music was constructed in layers rather than being the subject of an audio photograph or a phonograph. A performance is a unique event; recorded music, however, is not necessarily an exact mirror of a performance. Certainly that is how it began, but most contemporary recordings are the product of multitracking, multiple takes, sampled choruses, punched-in guitar solos – piecemeal sessions mixed together to form an end product. To some extent the recording process embodies an incestuous approach to the remix culture identified by Lawrence Lessig (2008) *et al.* Multitrack technologies – from reel-to-reel tape decks through to digital audio workstations – have revolutionized the way music was recorded.

Les Paul is frequently credited with pioneering what he called "sound on sound" recording, a technique that conceptually anticipated multitracking. Paul would cut a disc of his own performance and then record himself playing along with it, building a corpus of tracks culminating in a final master. Capitol Records released one recording that featured eight guitar tracks all played and recorded by Paul. In 1953, he privately commissioned Ampex to manufacture what would be the world's first eight track reel-to-reel tape recorder. The multitrack recorder differed technically from Paul's earlier experiments; the Ampex device allocated widths of the tape to individual recording and playback heads, thus allowing the recording of one track whilst simultaneously monitoring the other tracks. Two years later Ampex released the first commercially available multitrack recorders.

From the 1960s onwards multitracking became part and parcel of producing a record, but the term "record" is misleading:

> Only live recordings record an event; studio recordings, which are the great majority, record nothing. Pieced together from bits of actual events, they construct an ideal event. They are like the composite photograph of a minotaur. (Eisenberg 1987: 89)

Recordings no longer had to be made in a single unedited take. The benefit of recording in this manner is the isolation of each musical part from the others, allowing, for example, the vocals to be treated post-recording as a object distinct from the instrumental tracks. Some experiments in this area had already been successful using tape-splicing. Mark Katz (2010: 41) recounts attempts by the Beatles to record 'Strawberry Fields Forever' (1967). No complete rendition of the song was satisfactory to John Lennon, "but he did like the first half of Take 7 and Take 26". The two takes were in different keys and tempos, but by slowing down one and speeding up the other (an antecedent of what

DJs call "beat-mixing") George Martin was able to construct the final version. As Michael Chanan (1995: 142) notes, this approach to record production produced "records that seemed to be composed for the medium, rather than the medium transparently reproducing them".

While reel-to-reel multitrackers revolutionized the recording process, it was not until the late 1970s that such production technology became affordable for amateurs. Tascam released the Portastudio 144 in 1979, a revolutionary device offering four tracks on a standard compact cassette tape. As other companies such as Fostex, Marantz, Akai and Yamaha followed suit, multitrack recording reached the home studio. In the era before digital recording, the Portastudio and its competitors represented accessibility to the same recording techniques that had been limited to commercial studios since their inception.

Today, multitrack tape recording has been largely supplanted by digital audio workstations (DAWs). Computers running Cubase, Pro Tools, Ableton Live and Cakewalk Sonar offer recording, sequencing, editing and production tools for MIDI and audio. Whilst affordable, "pro" versions of multitrack software are still relatively expensive (Cubase and Pro Tools retail for many hundreds of dollars).

But cheaper alternatives exist – such as the open source and donation-funded Ardour package. The costs involved in setting up a modest home computer-based studio are now lower than ever, placing multitrack software, virtual synths, samplers, drum machines and other effects in the hands of professionals and amateurs alike.

Multitrack recording has many repercussions for music. The ability to record each track individually means that in the event of a bad performance only that track (or even a particular section of that track) needs to be re-recorded. Additionally, each track can be treated individually after the fact. This patchwork approach to recording helps reconstruct our understanding of music. Compared to a time in which recordings mirrored a live performance, the recorded artefact can be fabricated without the individual musicians ever being in the same place at the same time – a possibility that has been extended by contemporary computing and communications technologies.

Conclusion

The history of music technologies presented in this chapter is perhaps less detailed than those found in the texts of Chanan (1995), Eisenberg (1987), Katz (2010) and others, but providing a comprehensive history of recording was not our aim. We are concerned with highlighting the shifts and reconfigurations that occur when new technological opportunities are presented.

This chapter demonstrates that the music experience is not static, and during its short history has undergone significant changes that have coincided with technological developments and new ideas. The following two chapters emphasize how music is currently undergoing yet another change; how new technologies and new cultures are shaping each other.

2 Rise of the Machine

In 1995, the curmudgeon Clifford Stoll wrote a *Newsweek* opinion piece that dismissed the promise of networked computers as the hyperbole of "internet hucksters". He canvassed a range of popular activities and famously rejected the possibilities of the new media technologies:

> How about electronic publishing? Try reading a book on disc. At best, it's an unpleasant chore: the myopic glow of a clunky computer replaces the friendly pages of a book. And you can't tote that laptop to the beach. Yet Nicholas Negroponte, director of the MIT Media Lab, predicts that we'll soon buy books and newspapers straight over the internet. Uh, sure. (Stoll 1995)

In much the same way as the less-informed conflate short-term weather patterns with long-term climate trends, Stoll's is a classic misunderstanding of the dynamics of technological adoption. With the benefit of an extra fifteen years of hindsight, we can see that the digital computer evolved from being a massive mathematical machine to a personal media device – an evolution that coincided with the construction of a network that allowed those personal computers to "talk" to each other, enabling a range of new information and communication possibilities. The World Wide Web humanized that network, making the end points of use "people to people" (Laningham 2006). The resultant combination of information production, distribution and consumption devices not only forced traditional media institutions to reconsider their business methods and models, but also allowed a range of new media collaborations to emerge.

The previous chapter looked at changes in our understandings of, and relationships to, music. Whilst the majority of these changes coincided with the introduction of new technologies – printed sheet music, mechanical pianos, recording technologies and their artefacts – we argue that they were not solely determined by technological advances, but rather represented the confluence of techniques and ideas. This chapter extends the analysis to the current processes of technological change – the emergence of digital technologies and how they have enabled new ways of engaging with media in general, and music in particular.

Being Digital

Digital is a representational technology. It allows the codification of both the real and the imaginary using the basic building block of the binary number system – digital content is encoded numerically as a series of zeros and ones. All media forms can be represented digitally. Photographs, audio, video, graphics and text can all be digitized; their analogue forms are represented as digital files – coded combinations of zeros and ones that can be decoded into an analogue representation that allows us to perceive and engage with the material. Older technologies created media forms that were analogous to reality, miniature representations of actual life (old-fashioned film, for example, used a chemical process to trap reflected and refracted light), but digital technologies do something different. They codify representations of real life, by breaking down that continuous world into discrete, manageable numerical values. The technical processes involved are complex, but conceptually it is useful to think of digital as the recipe and analogue as the cake. Digitizing reduces the components of the cake into a codified set of instructions that allow it to be recreated by anyone who can interpret them. The advantages are clear: a recipe is much smaller and it's easier to modify, to copy, to communicate – it's much easier to send a recipe to grandma than an actual cake.

Compared to analogue forms, digital representations permit new possibilities of creativity and communication. Their numerical structure allows for easy mathematical manipulation. Most common of all is perhaps the (now humble) word processor, which has brought about a transformation in how we write. That manipulation of words with which we are so familiar (cutting, copying, pasting, endless rewriting, etc.) is now available across all media forms. A digital photograph, for example, is represented as a simple pattern of numbers. Digital tools allow relatively straightforward creation and manipulation of those images – and because the original pattern of numbers can be easily recalled (if saved!), the original form is never lost. Nowadays, any media form can be digitized, and then easily manipulated, stored, communicated and transmitted. The computer (in its broadest understanding) is the common centre of creative activity in media production facilities, whether textual, audio-visual or musical.

Word processors allow the shifting of words – totally reinventing the way writing happens. Image-manipulation tools like Photoshop allow seamless reshaping of magazine cover images. Sampling software means that old rock 'n' roll songs become part of hip-hop hits, and film is no longer cut and spliced with tape. Technologies of production that were rare and expensive are now far more affordable – and the available digital hardware and software are simplifying music production itself. Whereas multitrack recording in the analogue realm was fiddly and demanded highly developed technical skills, digital multitracking is more forgiving – manipulating tracks, whilst still requiring talent, is far less demanding. And even casual musicians can create professional-sounding songs with the assistance of clever tools ranging from Songify apps to the more sophisticated smart loops in apps like Apple's Garageband. Indeed, these newly accessible technologies of creation and manipulation have enabled what some argue is a democratization of production – more and more people can engage with media content in ways that were never before possible.

But lower cost and greater accessibility in production is not the only change in the digital media-scape; significant cultural provocations are also evident. Digital representations can be easily copied and stored for later reference. They are non-destructive, and do not suffer from generational decay, so Benjamin's (1992: 215) "aura" of an original has become less meaningful – unlike analogue copies, the third or fourth copy of a digital work is indistinguishable from the first. This is in stark contrast to an older medium such as magnetic tape that is affected by a degradation of quality with each generation of copy, and where even the original is at risk of damage each time it is played due to erosion of the lubricant applied to the tape (Van Bogart 1995: 9).

Additionally, the process of making digital copies requires little physical or mental effort and their electronic footprint is often minute when compared to the physical size of traditional information artefacts. Compare the affordances of digital music to examples of recorded music from the last chapter. The original cylinders are unimaginably cumbersome and fragile. Pianola scrolls were not much of an improvement, and vinyl recordings – whilst less delicate – were bulky, hard to transport and required careful handling of surface and stylus. Only two decades ago, we were still fiddling with cassettes and CDs, and although reasonably robust, they were limited as artefacts – containing only a dozen or so songs. Today, a typical portable mp3 player or smartphone offers storage space for more than 10,000 songs *in your pocket*.

Which, of course, leads to questions of how to manage and engage with so much music. Luckily, digital technologies can help us to cope. Computers are now powerful enough and software is intelligent enough to assist. So (in much the same way that Amazon recommends books based on our prior purchase and browsing activity), systems like the iTunes Genius function analyse our music libraries to create playlists and introduce us to new music based on our past listening experiences. Ever smarter search engines and streaming solutions such as Spotify make it easier to find music on the internet, and social networks provide hitherto impossible personal connections that turn word of mouth into a global activity.

All of the above possibilities have emerged because of continuous development in computing hardware that has evolved according to Moore's law (Moore 1965: 4–5) and doubled in power every eighteen months. Whilst the precise definition of this law refers to the density of microprocessor fabrication, the more generalizable observation is that all aspects of computing hardware have developed exponentially. This has allowed software to evolve just as quickly, taking advantage of increasingly powerful hardware.

Of course, computers by themselves represent only part of the picture. The other key development has been the connection of those computers. The development of computer-to-computer digital communication (Segaller 1998; Naughton 1999) has resulted in a global network of powerful computers through which information is exchanged almost instantaneously. The internet, the network of networks that has seen the connection of the vast majority of digital devices currently in use, has allowed the rapid transmission of information between those devices. What's more, the nature of the network means that dispersed communication between devices is as easy and as common as centrally controlled information flows and because digital bits can represent almost anything, all media forms – text, image, sound and video – once digitized can be easily transmitted worldwide. The many affordances of the internet have resulted in a radically transformed media- and music-scape.

Understanding the Internet

There are many ways to understand the internet; it exists not only as a complex technological network, but also as a cultural construct (Flew 2009: 58–79; Wardrip-Fruin 2003). At a technical level, the internet is a network of networks, defined by a particular set of protocols. A key technical approach to its understanding is the Open Systems Interconnection (OSI) model, which describes seven layers that make up the technical protocols of the Internet. At the base is the physical connection and at the top the application layer. The intermediate five layers are comprised of elements that control the data link, network, transport, sessions and presentation. The OSI model is a technical conceit – it sees the internet as a network and describes the various layering of technical requirements that allow information to flow. Although it is a limited way to understand the internet, technical definitions provide a basis to understand the social and cultural implications of the network.

The key distinguishing feature of the internet as a network is its architecture. It is built on an end-to-end principle of network design; the infrastructure (as articulated in most of the seven layers identified above) is technically simple and consistent and allows complex applications to be made by its end-users. The network layers simply carry the data, and what happens to that data at either end is up to users. So, end-users can easily innovate at the top layer (the application layer), knowing that their applications can communicate with other users across a consistent network.

And those applications are simultaneously looking towards the future and the past. In the media space, many radio, newspaper, television and music presences are nothing more than (sophisticated) internet applications seeking to replicate (and sometimes extend) older models of media dissemination. So radio and television networks host streams of their programme materials, newspapers post online the same stories that they publish in print and music labels sell music on CD or via digital download. In other words, the internet is malleable. It can, for example, be made to look just like a television, a video store or a place for global videotape swapping. Or, in the music domain, it can be made to look like a radio station, a record store or a giant repository of swappable mixed tapes. The key factor is not the technology, perhaps not even the uses to which that technology is put. The key factor is the overriding idea which informs it – and much of the Music 2.0 discussion centres on the opportunities (and challenges) that have arisen as a result of the internet's new affordances.

The media industries of the twentieth century were predicated on a key cultural idea – a flow of information and products that emanated outwards from an industry centre. The first media age (Holmes 2005: x) was characterized by the broadcast model – the notion of one-way transmission of content and programming by an active centre to peripheral dumb terminals. Programme development, broadcasting and consumption all occurred within a closed system entirely controlled by the industry in question. The key relationships were industry-to-industry and the late-twentieth-century dominance of a small number of large corporate interests in music and broadcasting was no surprise.

The combination of the personal computer (and its brethren) and the internet allows the reconfiguration of much traditional media practice. For example, it is now possible to discard the traditional vertical integration of production and distribution and decouple content production from distribution: book publishers no longer need printing presses or warehouses; television companies no longer require terrestrial networks or cable infrastructure; universities no longer require lecture theatres. Instead, they can focus on creating information products and use the internet for distribution. This allows for massive challenges to existing industries and the emergence of entities such as the iTunes Music Store, Amazon and Netflix, to name but a few. Additionally, entry barriers are lower – building a television application to stream content across the network is far less resource-intensive than building or negotiating access to a closed terrestrial, cable or satellite distribution system.

And, as we have seen, the power and accessibility of digital technologies is now such that the creation of internet applications is not the domain of a select few. So for individual musicians, distributing music no longer necessitates negotiations with labels and distributors. For example, Nine Inch Nails' front man Trent Reznor spent a month writing *The Slip* (2008) and just three weeks recording and producing it. He sent copies of 'Discipline' – the album's only single – via email to numerous radio stations within twenty-four hours of mastering the track, even before he had completed the remainder of the album.

Some argue that this widespread availability of technologies has resulted in a democratization of media and communications (Katz 1997), heralding a second media age (Holmes 2005: 4). An example of this is the blurring of the difference between the work of professionals and that of the amateur (Levy 1995: 216–19; Bruns 2008; Lessig 2008: 54–83). It is increasingly difficult to determine the origins of a particular work from its appearance, making superficial differences between individuals and institutions negligible. For example, an individual can produce a CD that would in no way look out of place on the shelf of a music retailer. Online music distribution takes that a step further and sets a quality baseline for professional and amateur alike.

More recently, the ubiquity of the smartphone and tablet – and the accessibility of application development and distribution tools – has seen the mobile app as the centre of much innovation. Examples in that space abound, many of which play with our engagements with music. Ocarina was an early iPhone app that allows users to make music (similar to a pan pipe) by blowing into the mouthpiece and fingering the notes. As well as being a cool, physical engagement with a technological device, Ocarina allows users to perform on a global scale; clicking a map of the world indicates the location of other Ocarina players whose performances can be heard with a simple tap. On a very small (and yet intrinsically large) scale, Ocarina represents the potential for internet users to create locally and perform globally. The sharing of music performance in the Ocarina app is mirrored by the broader ability of more substantial internet applications on any number of platforms.

Another miracle app for the mobile operating systems, Shazam, can be invoked to identify music being played and then suggest a means to (legally) obtain it. That song playing in a restaurant need no longer remain a mystery. Shazam "listens" to a snippet, compares its digital audioprint with a database of records, identifies the song and performer and links to various online retail stores for purchase. The point is not that these apps are innovative (even though they are). Rather they gesture towards a future for music that is built on the internet – where musical instruments, recording, performance, marketing, distribution, discovery and enjoyment are all internet-based.

This is intensified by the idea that digital technologies have all but eliminated the scarcity of information (although the implementation of this idea might venture into legally grey areas at times), which has been an issue largely due to the costs inherent in mass reproduction. Rather than a paucity of information, we now have the opposite. In an economy where scarcity has commodity value, a change from "atoms to bits" (Negroponte 1996: 4) has the potential to significantly alter ideas of commercial and cultural exchange.

Of course, such ideas have remained relatively utopian until recently. Until the end of the twentieth century, personal computers, let alone mobile phones, were incapable of living up to our imaginations, but bandwidth and processing power have increased enormously. Network communication speeds have also increased dramatically. Whereas internet data once flowed at a glacial pace, today's interconnecting networks now allow the transmission of information in an instant. And as computers have been getting more powerful and networks getting faster, the combined digital ecosystem has become more accessible.

The bandwidth – or capacity – of the network has also grown exponentially. The internet of the mid-1990s struggled to deliver still image files to domestically connected PCs. Today, many in the developed world can happily stream high-definition video onto their living-room screens. Moreover, just as technologies have become more affordable, significant progress has been made towards making the technologies invisible (Norman 1999). What some (such as Stoll) deride as impossible one moment, become new cultural habits the next. But those new cultural habits are not inevitable – the changes have been and continue to be contested.

The internet must be understood in that context. It is not merely the connection of computers on a TCP/IP network but the combination of creativity and communication that has created new information flows, new modes of media engagement and arguably new forms of media. As with the introduction of older media technologies such as radio and television, digital technologies provoked possibilities that are not intrinsic to their implementation. Such an "inevitable" promise of digital assumes a fixed, unevolving technological system – an approach that runs against historical precedent. An alternative understanding of the internet as a shifting and contested arena allows a more accurate view that counters determinist rhetoric and ultimately proves more useful and insightful. The internet should be understood as a battleground for competing ideas, not only technological ideas about protocols and connections, but also social and cultural ideas about how we create, disseminate and consume information and how those processes both affect and are affected by the ways in which we live. Indeed, we can identify some key contests in the history of music and the internet.

The Napster Moment

Napster saw the creation of a music-sharing network that grew from nothing to millions of users in less than a year (Mann 2000). In so doing, it threatened a number of existing institutions including the recording industry and undermined copyright laws. A successful lawsuit by the Recording Industry Association of America (RIAA) in the US Federal Court shut Napster down by imposing onerous operating conditions that effectively killed the service. The Napster case is a key example of the contested nature of the implementation of new media technologies. As a high-profile example of the successful control of "undesirable" information flows, it represented a very visible countering of the original "internet can't be regulated" trope (Chandrasekaran and Corcoran 1997). Moreover, it represented the overt restriction of the free flow of information using direct technical impositions invoked with the backing of common law. On the flipside, it exemplified the disruption that networked individuals can cause to hierarchical systems predicated on a twentieth-century broadcast model. Individuals have always shared recorded music whether through lending or copying. In the late twentieth century, the cassette tape was an enabling technology, and the creation of mix-tapes was a celebrated cultural habit of a generation, despite its legal uncertainty (Marshall 2005). Digital amplified those possibilities. Whereas the analogue mix-tape took supreme effort and was shared with a small circle of friends (or more likely with a single potential girl/boyfriend), Napster's affordances and ease of use took that activity – traditionally restricted to the private sphere – and expanded it to a potentially global scale, free of physical limitations.

Napster was about power and control in the new digital age. It questioned who controlled the commodity that is recorded music and opened up arguments about the competing rights of artists, record companies and consumers. Those who had power were determined to retain it against the interests of those who were enjoying their own moment of control. This shift in the locus of control was exemplified by a moment of theatricality in the Napster discourse. Metallica's entry into the anti-Napster camp led to vocal conflicts with its fan base. An exchange between drummer Lars Ulrich and an anonymous protester outside the Napster offices summed up the debate:

> Ulrich: We have the right to control our music!
> Voice from the crowd: Fuck you, Lars. It's our music too!
> (Mann 2000)

Here, competing ideologies are easily identified. Napster users (and they numbered in the tens of millions) resented the imposition of constraints on their cultural consumption. Bluntly, they resented their activities *as fans* being restricted by the very artists on whose albums, DVDs, T-shirts and performances they spent their money. As well as rejecting the economic constraint, Napster users were revelling in the freedom to reshape their music consumption experience to reflect their own subjectivities by building playlists to suit their own patterns of preference rather than one imposed by musicians, record producers or corporations. Addressing the cultural appropriation of trademarks, Alex Kozinski (1993: 975), a judge for the US Court of Appeals for the Ninth Circuit, posited:

> The originator of a trademark or logo cannot simply assert, 'It's mine, I own it, and you have to pay for it any time you use it.' Words and images do not worm their way into our discourse by accident; they're generally thrust there by well-orchestrated campaigns intended to burn them into our collective unconsciousness. Having embarked upon that endeavour, the originator of the symbol necessarily – and justly – must give up some measure of control. The originator must understand that the mark or symbol or image is no longer entirely its own, and that in some sense it also belongs to all those other minds who have received and integrated it.

At one level, Napster was practising high-tech *la perruque* on a global scale (de Certeau 1984: 29–42); the strategy of the CD as well as constructions of music that sit outside that of the commodified artefact were challenged by the tactic of digital file-sharing.

Of course, the outcome of the Napster case was the end of a particular file-sharing service. In effectively causing the demise of Napster, the courts reminded us that the invocation of new possibilities does not always result in the widespread adoption of a particular technological ideology. In this case, the "idea" of openness and free flows of information (that is, privileged by particular implementations of internet technology) was apparently beaten by the "idea" of control, akin to more traditional music-business models. But rather than disappear, the idea simply found other outlets – the reaction from users was to adopt other systems for music sharing, further evidence that technologies are arenas for the contestation of ideas and not fixed realms with immutable characteristics.

Web 2.0

In our discussion of the Napster moment, we alluded to the power of the personal computer and the internet to position each node or user as consumer *and* producer. This has been the case since the internet first emerged for public use – tropes such as "anyone can be a publisher" have hinted at the possibilities thrust into the mainstream with the so-called web 2.0.

The web 2.0 meme originated with publisher Tim O'Reilly (2005) at the end of the dot.com boom and was originally pointed towards the *business* of the internet. The idea was grounded in the observation, around 2003, that despite the bursting of the first dot.com bubble after March 2000, there were still successful new internet firms continuing to emerge. In the search for what these new firms had in common, the term "web 2.0" became common. It had an iconic moment of mainstream acceptance in Kevin Kelly's 2005 article in *Wired* magazine: "We Are the Web" and in *Time* magazine's 2006 cover story, which identified "you" as the Person of the Year.

The web 2.0 concept is most often applied to the idea of an online participatory culture, represented by the rise of blogging, file-sharing (photos, video and music), collaborative writing and editing, and social networks in the first decade of the new millennium (OECD 2007). The term has since been used to describe everything from the use of programming techniques such as AJAX, Google page-rank systems to popular websites that rely on tagging and recommendation, such as Flickr, Reddit and Digg. In his *Wired* piece, Kelly identifies a key theme in the web 2.0 discourse – the idea that "the producers are the audience, the act of making is the act of watching, and every link is both a point of departure and [a] destination". In many ways, the idea of web 2.0 is a more recent expression of what Tim Berners-Lee called "intercreativity" – "building together, being creative together" (Khare and Denison 1996).

Web 2.0 is perhaps best understood as a confluence of ideas and technologies that ease the processes of production, distribution and engagement. YouTube provides a salient example. In the early days of the web it was certainly possible to distribute video online, but it required a technical knowledge of digital video formats and how to set up a website and embed files for playback, something that was problematized by differences between operating systems and browsers. Today, however, an "out-of-the-box" software package such as Apple's iMovie features an export to YouTube option, after which the video-sharing site converts the uploaded file accordingly and provides a unique URL from which the video can be viewed via the web browser on a global scale. Indeed, contemporary smartphones take this one step further with YouTube uploads of video footage shot with the device's built-in camera available with a single touch.

In wider media analyses, the ease and accessibility of web 2.0 has led to discussions about the demise of journalism, attributed to the ever-increasing number of blogs that contribute to something that arguably resembles the ideal of a Habermasian public sphere. So-called user-generated content is celebrated by some. For example, Dan Gillmor argues that blogs exemplify a major shift in the news: "from journalism as lecture to journalism as a conversation or seminar" (2004: xiii). And Axel Bruns (2011) suggests that what some call "citizen journalists" can complement what he calls "industrial" journalism – by extending the breadth, the depth and the duration of coverage. By relocating editorial power to anyone with an internet connection, the constraints of twentieth-century media production are broken. But for the established news industry, the web 2.0 meme is part of an ongoing sense of crisis, as journalists need to reconsider their status and professional existence in a media-scape that has shifted from self-assigned fourth-estate status to simply another voice amongst many. Understandably, this reconfiguration of professions, an intrusion of the so-called "cult of the amateur" (Keen 2007), has led to aggressive debates.

It is easy to situate music in the centre of the web 2.0 maelstrom. The new technologies have enabled a number of significant shifts. The first is increased accessibility and a consumer expectation of on-demand digital delivery of the entire catalogue of musical offerings, legitimately or otherwise. The emergence of legitimate implementations of the "heavenly jukebox" (Mann 2000) is a clear response to today's 24/7 economies. Music buyers now demand the ability to obtain their tunes when they want, wherever they are – time and space are no longer seen as acceptable constraints. Importantly, where so-called legitimate services are unable to meet demand, then users turn to file-sharing services. For example, where old territorial copyright boundaries prevent music from being available globally, consumers refuse to be limited by what they see as irrelevant constraints, and simply go elsewhere for their instant gratification.

The second – and related – shift is a flattening of what was once a distinct divide between creator and audience. In the case of music, this flattening has two components. As well as musicians discovering new ways of engaging with their audiences, the audiences themselves are fast becoming collaborators in the act of musical production, as ideas of audience shift towards what Henry Jenkins calls participatory culture (2006: 290). This process encourages disintermediation – and the creation of a direct connection between musician and audience, not only via the traditional means of the music itself, but by creating different communications channels that largely bypass traditional middlemen (record labels, distributors, radio networks and independent record promoters). A consequence of this is the growing realization that the traditional manner of making money from music is no longer the only viable option.

The promise of Music 2.0, then, is nothing less than a possible reinvention of how musicians create, distribute and generate money from music (Draper 2007: 6–9). The characteristics of 2.0 combined with high-quality, low-bit-rate audio compression have shifted control away from record labels. In 1999 it would have been crazy for Nine Inch Nails or Radiohead to release an album online without a label, but that day is gone. The gateway between artist and audience is no longer the sole dominion of recording companies.

Digital technologies have evolved so that, speaking broadly, production is as easy or complex as the user demands; competencies aside, production technologies are accessible to the layperson. This has resulted in what has been called a "creative tsunami" (Aufderheide and Jaszi 2008: 2). Some of that creativity is strictly for self-consumption but some also seeks to find a wider audience through distribution. Of course, that desire to be public need not be one for global or even national prominence. Many individuals are content to be public in the school play, a website's chat room, or the family photo album. Others have a desire for celebrity, a need to be actualized or verified by appearing on national television (Rowe 2002). Whilst many home video users are happy to compile a collection of files on their hard drive, the more extrovert are determined that their efforts be broadcast at prime time. It is beyond the scope of this book to interrogate the motivations behind individual aspiration for fame and celebrity (Marshall 1997) but it is clear that many are willing to make their exploits public. Interviewees readily undergo vox pops or public humiliation at the hands of quiz or dating show hosts. The popularity of reality television is indicative not only of the desire by people to watch "real" people, but also of individuals to be seen.

Musicians are no different. Just as tools for creativity have become more accessible, internet technologies have made the process of publication easier and more accessible. By providing an affordable means of distribution – something that has traditionally been outside the domain of the average individual – the internet allows cheap, bidirectional communication of ideas with no deference to time or space. Suddenly, anyone who is a writer, artist, musician or film-maker can become a publisher and show his or her work to a large, potentially global audience for relatively small cost (Kenner 1999). Of course, the technical means of production and distribution do not automatically bring audiences, influence or power but this is another step in the flattening of traditional media hierarchies and opens up other avenues for communication. In short, the internet has allowed for a publishing space: a realm for exploration and experimentation.

It would be remiss to assume that prior to the opportunities provided by the internet the only creative efforts were those publicized by the publishing gatekeepers of the twentieth century. But the Net has expanded the scope for publication. Put simply, the internet provides an opportunity for the hidden to be seen, for the vernacular to occupy a space previously reserved for those chosen by the traditional gatekeepers.

It would also be a mistake to attribute a single mode of usage to the internet. Whilst the idea of empowerment expressed in innumerable intercreative acts may be common, such acts are not descriptive of every user. The internet's huge user-base suggests a diversity of uses that cannot be reduced to a monolithic unity of purpose. We suggest that uses of the internet can only exist within a framework of possibilities; that technology (as articulated in the previous chapter) defines the broad parameters within which users express their desires. In this understanding, uses of the internet are broadly confined within an assemblage that itself is shaped not only by technical means, but also by confining cultural means, which include policy and economic interventions. It cannot be stressed often enough that the internet is constantly being shaped and that contests over its cultural intent are aimed precisely at the type of uses that it may allow.

In effect, the contest is between traditional models of media usage and their adherents – namely, large media organizations, and to a lesser extent governments – and newer models of usage that privilege and empower the user. Arguably, the contest was originally skewed by a culture of openness and freedom inscribed into the early internet by a combination of invisible subsidy and opportune cultural moment. The key question remains as to the extent that culture is still essential to the internet experience, and consequently to what extent attempts to impose models of control are hindered by not a technological but a cultural mode of resistance. In short, does the network aesthetic overwhelm any ideology of centralized control in the evolution of the technical system that is the internet? And is it possible for different modes of operation to co-exist? Is there continuity alongside transformation?

Convergence?

In the previous chapter we suggested that the mere presence of technology is insufficient to provoke change. Rather, the affordances of the new technologies will enable possibilities that provoke a contest over change. The connected personal computer in its various incarnations has ushered in that particular contest, and as a result all information industries are grappling with the changes.

The internet has brought about the disruption of traditional business models; media forms have seen their revenue streams hijacked by alternative distribution mechanisms. Just as the newspaper industry, for example, has seen its historical revenue stream of classified ads stolen by more efficient online listings, so the recorded music business is under threat from the much more efficient distribution of digital files. Combined with the internet's low barriers to entry that have empowered a range of new content providers, there is the temptation to dismiss formerly dominant companies as nearly extinct dinosaurs. The reality is far from that simple; large corporations still possess the resources to wield significant power; there remain influential media organizations with the ability to shape the industry, create fame and popularize musicians who can command huge audiences. But the traditional record labels have had to do business with Silicon Valley, and the industry now relies on companies such as Apple, Amazon and Google to engage with its audiences. This is nothing new – record labels have maintained relationships with hardware manufacturers and radio networks in the past – but the shifting nature of the industries is telling; the cultures of computing and content companies can often be at odds.

In 2007 *Wired* magazine featured a revealing interview with Doug Morris (Mnookin 2007). Now the chairman and CEO of Sony Music Entertainment, Morris served Universal Music Group in the same roles between 1995 and 2011. The interview highlighted the cultural contest over the construction of music. The recording industry was founded on the commodification of the recorded artefact; the transition (initially led by the audience) to digital files, free of physical media, was one with which record labels struggled to cope. In the same article, Ted Cohen, a former executive at EMI and Warner Brothers, states, "They [record labels] wouldn't let go of CDs"; instead of exploiting the new media to their advantage, the labels aggressively turned on the emergent new distribution networks. For an industry so focused on marketing a recorded artefact, intangible digital files represented an unknown enemy, and the industry was totally unprepared. Morris recounts:

> There's no one in the record company that's a technologist. That's
> a misconception writers make all the time, that the record industry
> missed this. They didn't. They just didn't know what to do.

In the next chapter we deal more specifically with how this knowledge void was filled by partnerships with computer companies.

Beyond the new industrial convergences that emerged, the new technologies enabled the convergence of one-to-one and one-to-many communications, resulting in hybrid forms; social networks have blurred the distinction between distribution and communication; what exactly are music bloggers doing when they upload an mp3 file? And how does a Facebook "Like" fit with established models of music criticism? The answer is "somewhere in between" and the role of social media in the music realm is clearly a site of struggle. The phenomenal early success of MySpace was built largely on the network of connections it enabled – musicians and fans, fans and fans, musicians and musicians. Facebook, MySpace's apparent heir, appears to be less music-centric, but clearly represents an opportunity for musicians and fans alike to connect in previously impossible ways. The emergence of embeddable external media such as YouTube videos or the SoundCloud widget further accentuates the possibilities.

Of course, there are trade-offs in the blurring of private and public – the persistence and accessibility of the data shared on Facebook and its ilk challenge accepted social conventions as previously private communications take on public elements and vice versa. Users find themselves negotiating new terrain but those tensions have not reduced the popularity of social networks. At the time of writing, Facebook boasts in excess of a billion active users, an achievement that leads some to suggest its expanding platform is the new centre of the web (Kirkpatrick 2010: 373–5) and perhaps the centre of music. At the F8 Developers Conference on 22 September 2011, Mark Zuckerberg announced his intention to more tightly integrate multiple music services into Facebook's operation in an attempt to break down the barriers separating individual models (Protalinski 2011). In 2013, Facebook incorporated numerous music services including TuneIn, MOG, Spotify and SoundCloud.

Another key convergence is that of media texts themselves. Like other media forms, music finds itself mashed-up, remixed, reinvented and re-purposed. It is the soundtrack for teenage antics on YouTube videos or juxtaposed in innovative forms (a favourite of the authors being 'Smells Like Teen Booty', which emerged from the collision of Nirvana and Destiny's Child). Kutiman takes it to a new level by sourcing user-generated contents from YouTube and combining them into new ensembles. 'My Favourite Color' (2011) was compiled from twenty-two existing videos of original instrumental tracks overlaid with vocals provided by Tenesan1, a YouTube contributor, singing her own unaccompanied composition into her webcam. Reflecting the "found sound" aesthetic of *musique concrète*, as of March 2013 'My Favourite Color' had been viewed by over 800,000 YouTube users, featured on the front page of Reddit and voted favourite music video on the YouTube channel. Similarly, the Gregory Brothers mix their own musical talents with media culled from the news in their "Auto-Tune the News" project. The 'Backing Up Song' (2010) – which culled its vocals from an eyewitness report of a convenience store robbery – was a viral hit, spawned numerous cover versions and merchandise, and led to Songify, an "auto-tune yourself" iPhone app. The song is available for free on YouTube or can be purchased from iTunes. The profits are split between the Gregory Brothers and Diana Radcliffe, the eyewitness who unwittingly provided the vocals.

John Hartley asks, "Is it possible to tell a society by how it edits?" (2000: 44) and perhaps the new media technologies afford the emergence of an edit culture with the ability to distribute these new cultural objects on a global scale. It is little surprise that what has emerged is a widespread implementation of the mash-up model, in which texts are remixed and reimagined in ways that their original authors could not have envisaged.

Of course, there is a historical precedent to this type of musical activity. When music was primarily built around performance, then musicians themselves brought their own expression to published sheet music – and interpretations of particular songs varied from performance to performance. Toynbee (2006: 78) argues that the dominant mode of music-making in the twentieth century was that of "phonographic orality" – whose earliest manifestation can be seen in the way that jazz and blues musicians built their repertoire through listening and reconfiguring. He builds on Walter Ong's (1982: 133) notion of "secondary orality" to argue that folk modes of creativity based on repetition and variation – drawn from listening to existing musical artefacts – are a normal part of modern music composition. Arguably, Hartley's edit culture (2000: 44) is an expression of this trait – and, as ever with the internet, has been amplified in its scale, scope and visibility by the affordances of the new technologies.

Because music has always been implicated in technological development, it is impossible to imagine the production and dissemination of music without the use of some technological system. It is no surprise that it was, in many ways, the guinea-pig sector and was dealt the first blows by digital technologies. Late-twentieth-century implementations were constrained by processor power and bandwidth, two factors that limited the size of files that could be manipulated and shared. These limitations largely protected video from early digital experiments, while print publishing was tied to a portable document format whose advantages, until relatively recently, were difficult to replace with screens. Music was the perfect target – digitization was relatively simple and provided cost and convenience advantages to users with few downsides. The next chapter explores the key moments in music's shift to the brave new (digital) world.

3 Digital Music

In his 1997 book *The Innovator's Dilemma*, Clayton Christensen coined the phrase "disruptive technologies" to describe those which often enter at the bottom of the market, where they are ignored by established players. These technologies then grow in power and sophistication to the point where they eclipse the old systems (Christensen 1997: 129). The idea has become a somewhat overused cliché, cited by business-school entrepreneurial types whenever they pitch anything they wish to sell for a squillion dollars to a venture capital firm. But the story of digital music – and more specifically digital music on the internet – arguably revolves around a disruptive technology that allowed users to work around the constraints of a slow network and less-than-powerful computer hardware. That technology – the mp3 file format – allowed the creation of music files that, despite sounding inferior to CD audio, could be shared using the relatively slow transfer rates of the turn-of-the-millennium internet. This good-enough approach triggered a tsunami of activity by users keen to explore digital music on the internet – proof of concept for new entrants in the music game, a visible threat to existing record labels and the impetus for reinventing the business of music. A decade later, the technical limitations have largely disappeared, and music files are no longer as highly compressed, but the mp3 format clearly triggered ongoing disruption.

The previous chapter explained the context of the broader digital shift and introduced some key contests. The networked digital computer affected many industries, and music was not immune; in many ways the experiences of the music industries foreshadowed the tensions and opportunities available for other sectors of content production. This chapter explores digital music in more detail, examining the shift to digital distribution and how that has reshaped the existing music industry.

At the end of the twentieth century, a particular combination of demographic and format provoked a challenge to traditional music-industry practices that continues to this day. Although piracy and file-sharing networks are an integral part of the back story to digital music, they are not the focus of this chapter and will share this space with an examination of the emerging opportunities afforded to musicians – professional and amateur, signed and unsigned. In Chapter 1, we characterized the development of recorded music through its relationship to space and time through recording, duplication and layering. This chapter addresses a final dimension – distribution. Whilst earlier technological developments enabled musicians to reconfigure space and time, those outside the recording industry were stymied by an inability to distribute their music on a wide scale. Arguably, in terms of breaching the monopoly forged by the recording industry, reconfiguring distribution was a *coup de grâce* – and one that evolved completely outside of that industry's control.

In hindsight, it is unsurprising that the distribution of music was so easily disrupted. Firstly, music lovers had long subverted the centrally maintained control that the major labels had on content production and distribution; home recording, mix tapes, bootleg recordings and, more broadly, *sharing* have been part of musical cultures since recording technologies became widely accessible. Music sharing was already a cultural habit long before the PC and the internet arrived. Marshall (2005: 108–9, 114–16) documents the difficulties of closing the loopholes exploited by bootleggers in the 1980s, as well as the emergence of Bob Dylan's *Great White Wonder* (1969) bootleg. Laing (2003: 489) reports that by the early 1970s the music industry was alarmed by the degree of home taping and that 80 to 90 percent of blank cassettes sold were used for private copying.

Secondly, pop music tends to be a young person's realm, and that same demographic is over-represented in the early-adopter, digital-native space. A love for music and a love for playing with new digital tools frequently go hand in hand. Whilst the term "digital native" might best be understood as a mindset, rather than a generational descriptor, younger people do tend to embrace new technologies. For example, Pew survey data show that so-called "millennials" tend to be more mobile with their gadgets and are the group with the biggest adoption of mp3 players; for example, in the 2011 Pew survey, 74 per cent of 18- to 34-year-olds owned an mp3 player (Zickuhr 2011: 2).

Thirdly, by the time internet connections became common in the home, music was already digital: in the 1980s, the industry introduced the compact disc, which provided manufacturing and distribution efficiencies and allowed labels to re-market existing recordings in a new format on the premise of greater fidelity, ease of use and longevity. The unintended consequence of that format shift from analogue vinyl LP to digital plastic CD was the ease with which the digital CD integrated into the personal computer/internet ecosystem. Unlike the days of home taping on cassette, a CD's digital content could be copied and redistributed in less than real time. The CD was also the successor to the floppy disk, the new purveyor of information and entertainment.

The particular combination of a sharing culture, a technologically savvy demographic and ready availability of musical source material represented a perfect storm. But that perfect storm did not emerge spontaneously.

The internet of the 1990s lacked bandwidth, and the personal computer of the same period was not particularly powerful. Processing digital files (while more efficient than copying cassettes) was still time-consuming and resource-intensive. The accelerated adoption of alternative music distribution through file sharing via websites or peer-to-peer networks can be attributed to other developments, primarily methods for compressing large audio files into something more manageable by the bandwidth available to most home users.

MP3

It could be argued that this music revolution was brought to you by the letters M and P and the number 3. MP3 is a format for compressing large audio files into smaller ones. Clever algorithms remove parts of the audio without significantly damaging the quality, achieving a compression ratio of roughly twelve to one. Exactly how the compression works is beyond the scope of this book; we are more interested in the whys and hows of MP3's popularity and the concomitant impacts on the cultures of consumption and production (see Sterne 2012).

The popularity and dominance of MP3 as the digital music format of choice is, to some extent, the result of fortuitous timing. MP3 is shorthand for MPEG Audio Layer-3. The result of research by a German scientific research group, the Fraunhofer Society, the compression technique was intended to reduce audio file size while remaining as true to the original, uncompressed version as possible. Although some Fraunhofer researchers such as Dieter Seitzer had been investigating compression methods since the mid-1970s, it was the work of Seitzer's student, Karlheinz Brandenburg, that bore fruit (Sterne 2012: 112). Seitzer and his research group at Fraunhofer were researching the optimum method for transmitting high-quality audio over a standard telephone line, and this is what eventuated. Seitzer could not have predicted that the research would result in millions of digital music files being exchanged between Napster users who were using the telephone line system as the primary vehicle for transmission.

The Motion Picture Experts Group (MPEG) of the International Standards Organization (ISO) was charged with developing compressed digital audio and video standards. Fraunhofer was not alone; other universities and research groups were also in the race to create high-quality, low-bit-rate audio compression that would gain approval from MPEG. In 1993, lengthy discussion and some consolidation resulted in the MPEG-1 compression standard for digital video. Its audio section sets out three layers of codecs. Layer 3 is the most efficient, capable of the highest compression-to-quality ratio. Following an internal poll at Fraunhofer in 1995, .mp3 was voted the file extension to be used for files produced by Fraunhofer's MP3 encoding software L3enc (Layer-3 encoder) (Fraunhofer Institute for Integrated Circuits n.d.). Two months later, Fraunhofer released the Winplay3 real-time software MP3 player for the Window platform. Given that in the mid-1990s average hard-drive capacity was somewhere between 500 and 1000MB, a compression method like MP3 was essential to store any significant amount of digital audio on a computer. Additionally, domestic internet bandwidth was limited. Compression techniques allowed the transmission of data more easily; even with today's much larger bandwidth, file compression is useful to ensure efficient carriage of big digital files. Whether it is zipping up a collection of high-resolution images to email or watching a video on YouTube, the ability to reduce file sizes can still be a priority – particularly on mobile networks. The MP3 codec emerged at a time when the average user's internet speed and data limits precluded the transfer of music files in their native, uncompressed format.

What happened next was the start of an unpredicted revolution, but in hindsight the results of releasing a music-compression tool designed to transmit high-quality audio files across telephone lines were unsurprising. MP3 compression was key in facilitating distribution of digital music. Websites, peer-to-peer file sharing and an avalanche of supporting software spurred discovery and widespread adoption of not only the format but also the concept of digital (artefact-free) music itself.

MP3 is not the only digital music format, but it certainly occupies a special place in music history as the one that irrevocably changed music. Its compression ratio is optimal for sharing via the internet and has made distribution of music easy and accessible to all. MP3 contributed to a reconfigured understanding of music consumption, production and distribution. Small hard-drive capacities and slow internet connection speeds made the format perfect for a generation that spent increasing amounts of time in front of a computer listening to music while gaming or on forums and chat. Further, it coincided with a golden age in home recording afforded by the personal computer. Just like the fans, musicians were also spending increasing amounts of time in front of a computer using digital multitrack software to produce high-end recordings on a par with those coming out of major-label-funded studio sessions. Whilst the compact cassette and CD provided some measure of distribution for the unsigned musician, the production process was laborious and without institutional support distribution at an industrial level was nearly impossible. MP3, however, provided an incredibly cost-effective – not to mention *unprecedented* – way to distribute music.

MP3.com

In the latter half of the 1990s the uptake of MP3 grew exponentially. The ready availability of accessible digital music files spawned personal computer software that enabled their simple playback and distribution. Websites and other internet services emerged to cater for the demand for MP3 files. It did not take the format long to gain popularity and not long after its adoption by users, fans demonstrated that there was a market for music free of an artefact, albeit underground.

Nullsoft released its first version of Winamp (a program which allowed users to play and organize their mp3 files) in 1997 and shortly afterwards mp3.com began offering thousands of songs by unsigned artists. The desire to discover and acquire music via the network was noted when Greg Flores saw the search-term logs for filez.com, an File Transfer Protocol (FTP) service operated by himself and Michael Robertson. Both were impressed by the audio quality of uploaded files and quickly invested in purchasing the mp3.com domain name from Martin Paul. Flores stated during an interview that within the first 24 hours www.mp3.com had redirected over 18,000 unique hits to filez.com and companies such as Zing Technology were keen to purchase advertising space on the site (Warner 2010).

Mp3.com did not arise out of a vacuum, but was the culmination of several initiatives involving the MP3 format and online distribution up to that point. Flores and Robertson noticed that there was a loose network of individuals sharing MP3 files. The files being shared were predominantly ripped from CDs, but mp3.com tapped into the blurring of production and consumption and took advantage of the ease with which all users could be participants – as producers and consumers of content, or even as new intermediaries by aggregating and distributing digital content. All of a sudden, there were far fewer constraints on participation as the walls that had sheltered and privileged the recording industry were breached. The nascent characteristics of web 2.0 meant that unsigned artists could gain access to audiences. Online music distribution sites arrived and operated outside the domain of the established industry.

In that environment, mp3.com provided two major developments to the emerging field of digital music. First, artists could upload their own music and distribute it via the site as downloads, streaming audio and Digital Automatic Music (DAM) CDs. Second, it provided the more consumer-oriented MyMP3 or Beam It service.

In its early days, unsigned and independent musicians spanning all genres colonized mp3.com. After signing up, each artist was given a profile page and unique URL, such as www.mp3.com/infest8. As with its more recent successor

MySpace, profile pages could be easily customized and music in MP3 format uploaded and distributed via download and/or streaming. For musicians, the attraction was that the site did all the work; they did not have to concern themselves with learning HTML and cross-browser MP3 playback, securing web hosting and domain name registration. Indeed, mp3.com was a seminal web 2.0 property – providing tools that enabled ordinary, non-geek users to participate in the internet and wider music production culture. It pioneered self-publishing of music in the same way that blogs provided an outlet for writers.

Sign-up was easy and the distribution infrastructure was already in place. For the first time unsigned musicians had easy access to a wider audience. Visibility and attracting attention were still factors, but the gates to the audience that had been the dominion of the recording industry were being kicked open by an alternative model to that which had dominated since the commercialization of recording technologies. In addition to offering music via streaming and downloads, mp3.com's artists could produce CDs by selecting from their uploaded tracks and artwork. Unlike the traditional approach to supply and demand, so-called DAM CDs were burned and mailed out on an on-demand basis, with no stock overheads. The retail price of a DAM CD was usually in the region of US$7, with a small percentage allocated to mp3.com to cover production costs. The DAM CDs could be played in conventional hi-fi CD players but also held MP3 versions of the same tracks.

DAM CDs were an important challenge – at least conceptually, if not in terms of volume – to the established recording industry. Independent and unsigned artists could potentially make money from their music without all the middlemen and contracts involved in the traditional process. Between 1999 and 2001 portable mp3 players were not commonplace, but the inclusion of MP3 versions of the audio tracks on a DAM CD acknowledged an emergent shift in music consumption culture towards a product free of a physical artefact.

In mid-1999 mp3.com opened for public investment and raised in excess of US$370 million; at the end of that year a "payback for playback" (P4P) scheme was launched to pay artists according to the number of unique streams and downloads, with the pool of P4P funds generated from on-site advertising. In addition to providing a revenue stream to artists, P4P forced those artists serious about making money to look beyond the potentials of the new distribution network in reaching the audience and to engage with the perennial problem of attention. Whether through an online music distributor, a personal website or blog, or via YouTube, anyone could release music online, but the real challenge was getting noticed. As Andrew Dubber puts it,

> making a webpage, putting it online and expecting people to read
> it is a bit like writing a book, sticking it in the library – and then
> coming back a year later only to wonder why nobody had ever
> checked it out. (2007: 32)

Mp3.com's P4P scheme rewarded the high-flyers of the attention economy with hard cash – and there are clear cases of it working. For example, the Cynic Project (aka Alex Smith) earned US$4789 in January 2000 alone (Spellman 2002: 61). Together with CD sales and further P4P monies, Smith earned in excess of $125,000 in two years on mp3.com. Similarly, during the summer of 2000, Mikel Fair and Jordan Kolar of 303Infinity embarked on a promotion campaign in which flyers with the band's mp3.com URL were distributed up and down the beaches of California. This campaign resulted in a period where 303Infinity was earning an impressive US$700 per day and netted around $250,000 from P4P across four years. In Mikel Fair's own words,

> the Payback for Playback program means that I can dedicate myself
> 100 per cent to my music. MP3.com has given me a way to skip the
> middle man, communicate directly with my fans and become suc-
> cessful without the daunting need for nationwide radio play and
> distribution. (*Billboard*, 8 July 2000)

These early examples of disintermediation foreshadowed the many opportunities the future had to offer.

Of course, not every artist was making money on this scale, but for many financial gain was not the motivating factor. For the amateur or hobbyist musician, mp3.com represented a connection between musician and (potential) audience, an opportunity to be heard by others outside the immediate local and/or social circle. Although this connection was unprecedented, it is important to stress that online music distribution suited some forms of music better than others. Whilst mp3.com certainly hosted some classical music, the production costs of recording an orchestra (at least using real instruments) outstripped those of the bedroom electronic artist.

Online distribution was complemented by the emergence of accessible music production technologies. Digital Audio Workstation (DAW) software such as Cubase and the VSTi (Virtual Studio Technology instrument) are used in both professional and amateur studios, but for the amateur musician affordable software severely reduces the costs of production. With a sufficiently powerful computer and soundcard, music producers can easily put together a home studio. Equal access to the tools of production and distribution removed any discrimination between amateur bedroom production, professional studio production and everything in between. Obviously, this claim is subject to some qualification. The democratizing functions of digital technology and the network are prone to hyperbole: simply owning the necessary production software does not automatically make you sound like Mark Ronson, any more than owning a guitar guarantees you'll play like Hendrix.

Some amateurs have the budget to record in a studio and use online music distribution channels to reach their audience. Similarly, professional artists signed to major labels can use the same channels. In its early days mp3.com featured mostly amateur musicians attracted to the site's DIY aesthetic, but by the turn of the century, major-label artists started to have a presence. The result of mp3.com's open-door policy was the occupation of the site's charts by established artists offering songs for free download or streaming. The presence of established artists such as Astral Projection – which has always released music from its own label, but is still one of the world's premiere trance acts – clogged the charts and pushed many amateur artists away from the opportunities for exposure.

In many ways, mp3.com was years ahead of its time, a factor that most likely contributed to its demise (at least in its then incarnation) in 2001. Despite its importance to the digital music revolution, its history was littered with legal issues stemming from the site's Beam It or MyMP3 service, which launched in early 2000. Thousands upon thousands of CDs ripped to MP3 format were offered for streaming playback, providing users could prove (via the service's verification procedure) that they owned a copy of the original CD. Beam It foreshadowed the current movements in cloud-based music, but rather than a subscription-based model, users only had access to music they had already purchased.

The recording industry was already wary of digital copying because of Napster. Universal Music Group launched a successful legal action against mp3.com, but ultimately entered into an out-of-court settlement in which it licensed its entire music portfolio to mp3.com for $53.4 million. Beam It was discontinued in mid-2001 after a financially crippled mp3.com was sold to Vivendi Universal. Although Beam It was oriented for consumer music rather than DIY artists, the initiative demonstrated a demand for accessibility to digital music beyond the CD. Further, it also demonstrated the reluctance of the major recording labels to allow developments in the industry outside of their control.

Michael Robertson's original mp3.com died in 2003 after Vivendi's difficulties in expanding the service. CNET bought the domain name and established its own distribution service and partnered with Last.FM in 2009. Naturally, mp3.com was not the only music distribution service that emerged on the web. Just as a cohort of other file-sharing networks joined Napster, at the turn of the century mp3.com shared the stage with a number of contemporaries. What is interesting about these sites is that at this stage in time the MP3 (or any artefact-free digital format) had not been successfully monetized on the scale that we know it today. In some ways, mp3.com's model mirrored that of radio – music was used to direct consumer attention to advertisers and the physical CD – with the point of departure being that mp3.com was accessible without record-label patronage.

Peoplesound

UK-based (and now defunct) Peoplesound.com took a different approach from mp3.com. Whereas mp3.com had an open-door policy that allowed anyone to upload music of any compositional and production quality, Peoplesound's approach was reminiscent of the traditional recording labels, requiring artists to submit a CD or mini-disc which would be scrutinized for quality by its eight full-time A&R staff and a loose network of freelancers. In *New Musical Entrepreneurs*, Paul Brindley cites Ernesto Schmitt, the founder of Peoplesound, referring to the site as "an interim record company" (2000: 49). Peoplesound used mp3s as promotional material to sell CDs from which the company took a 50 per cent cut. At the 2000 Record Producers Guild meeting in Nomis Studios, London, the discussion centred on the future of record companies in the light of emerging online music distribution websites. Stefan Heller, Peoplesound's A&R and Programming Director, spoke at length on how companies such as Peoplesound were going to revolutionize the record industry, based on the cyberspace adage that anyone can be a publisher, and said that traditional record companies were about to become extinct in the wake of a democratized model of music distribution. Of course, traditional record companies have not become extinct (or at least not at the time of writing), but Peoplesound has folded.

The interesting thing about Peoplesound is that it took on a far more active role than mp3.com, which merely set up its infrastructure, attracted content, and did very little to promote its music portfolio. Peoplesound, in contrast, was modelled as an online record company. Mp3.com leaned more towards a disintermediation of the distribution process and Peoplesound more towards a remediation. Its A&R process scrutinized submissions and actively recruited new talent. Larraine Segil reveals that Peoplesound had "1,000 talent scouts in rehearsal rooms, avenues – wherever artists are found or heard" (2001: 186). Further, Peoplesound invested in its artists. For example, relationship managers worked with the top hundred artists to get record deals and compilation CDs were given away with national newspapers. In April 2000 Peoplesound announced the launch of a b2b (business-to-business) licensing arm to promote its portfolio to advertisers. Thus, Peoplesound established itself as a more business-minded venture than mp3.com, which despite its commerciality leaned more towards a participatory community. Peoplesound was marking the future for a new type of music-business intermediary.

Whilst admittedly short-lived, the success of mp3.com, Peoplesound and other contemporaries such as Ampcast and Vitaminic was apparent in connecting music fans with the masses of unsigned or amateur musicians of every genre. The vast majority of such musicians were not going to retire off their pay-for-play funds or revenue from CD sales, but for them the appeal of participation was the ability to distribute their music.

The Majors – So Sue Me?

Whilst new companies were exploring the opportunities afforded by cheap digital distribution, existing institutions could see nothing but a threat to their existing business practices. Established record companies were driven by profit – their survival depended on generating sufficient revenue and their business model was based on signing acts in the hope of sales success or, at the very least, ensuring that their successful artists in terms of sales outnumbered their failures. Record labels have traditionally had a direct financial stake in the creativity and marketability of their signings. This is a clear differentiator from online music distributors, which did not advance money to artists. Marketability was not an issue because there was little financial risk, and experience with the web has demonstrated that there is a market for almost everything (albeit sometimes very small). Online distributors derived their income from numerous sources such as the sale of physical and digital media, merchandise, advertising and subscriptions to premium services. In their early days, online distributors primarily dealt with the unsigned or amateur artist in a growing market which called for digital music that was not (legally) being fulfilled by the major labels.

For established labels, entities like mp3.com and Peoplesound posed little threat. Their online distribution models did not impinge on the core business of the majors. However, the internet enabled other activities, which did.

The same year that online music distribution was levelling the playing field for musicians, Napster emerged: the peer-to-peer software package that would change the music industry forever. Between June 1999 and July 2001 the peer-to-peer Napster stirred the tension between the MP3 format and the Record Industry Association of America (RIAA). File sharing was already occurring through Internet Relay Chat (IRC), USENET and FTP servers, but had largely gone unnoticed by the recording industry and less tech-savvy computer users. However, Napster's user-friendly interface and dedication to music made it easy for fans to download free audio files. As discussed in the previous chapter, Napster enabled – or, at least, enabled on a large scale – an entirely different model of engagement with music. The music industry would term that engagement "piracy" but others would argue that it is impossible to determine fans' primary motivations for downloading music en masse via Napster. At its peak, Napster was directing 25 million users to 80 million songs. It is clear that a variety of motives were in play. Some users were interested in acquiring bootlegs or obscure recordings no longer in circulation. After already purchasing music on vinyl or cassette, some users felt justified in downloading a format-shifted version. Others simply enjoyed accumulating music for free and discovering new songs and artists; for those it played the role of radio for the internet generation.

But the established music industry clearly saw a threat. In the middle of its short life, Napster incurred the wrath of Metallica following their sudden awareness that a demo of 'I Disappear' (2000) was being propagated across the internet, along with the rest of the band's back catalogue. And, more than just for "personal use", the demo was also being played on radio stations across the USA. Metallica (later joined by Dr Dre) filed suit against Napster. A separate action by the RIAA in the same year sued Napster for contributory and vicarious copyright infringement. The US Court of Appeals for the Ninth Circuit affirmed and remanded the case to the District Court, where Napster was ordered to filter its service and block access to an enormous number of nominated copyrighted songs. Designed to facilitate the free and unhindered discovery and sharing of music, Napster was unable to censor itself and ceased service in 2001.

Taking out the distribution network proved that digital distribution could be controlled; apparently, the RIAA had won. However, since Napster's demise a torrent of successors and alternatives, legal and otherwise, presented themselves. As with the mythical Lernaean Hydra, cutting off one head merely sprouted two more. If attacking the network didn't work, then targeting users might.

The RIAA continued on a litigious pathway, suing both individuals and companies that attracted its wrath. In 2003 the recording industry launched 4280 lawsuits against music fans for sharing music in the wake of Napster – a civil assault against an unprecedented number of people. The RIAA alleged, and still maintains, that file sharing negatively affects its profits, that every download is a lost sale. In 2003 Sony BMG's Head of Litigation, Jennifer Pariser, went so far as to say, "When an individual makes a copy of a song for himself, I suppose we can say he stole a song. 'Making a copy' of a purchased song is just a nice way of saying 'steals just one copy'" (Bangeman 2007). The

Electronic Frontier Foundation reports that in the five years between 2003 and 2008 the recording industry had "filed, settled, or threatened legal actions against at least 30,000 individuals".

The results of this campaign included calls to boycott the RIAA, counterclaims and much negative publicity focusing on the ruin brought to the everyday lives of single mothers, grandparents and students by multinational companies. The lawsuits and contentious use of private enforcement companies received a great deal of publicity; much of it has been negative (EFF 2008). For example, consider the cases of Jammie Thomas (now Thomas-Rasset) and Joel Tenenbaum. In 2007 Thomas was sued for copyright infringement stemming from file sharing twenty-four songs, with the RIAA demanding $222,000 ($9250 per song). Because of an error during the hearing, a new trial by jury was held in 2009, after which the RIAA was awarded $1.92 million in damages. The judge reduced the damages to $54,000, a sum rejected by the RIAA. On appeal in 2010 a jury awarded $1.5 million to the recording industry, which once again was reduced to $54,000 ($2250 per song). Whilst these sums may appear (to quote Judge Michael Davis, who presided in Thomas's 2009 case) "monstrous and shocking" and suggest a "gross injustice", the RIAA, driven by compensatory and punitive motives (Anderson 2010), sought statutory damages and appealed yet again. In September 2012 an Eighth Circuit Court of Appeals found in favour of the RIAA, reinstated the original damages of $222,000 and imposed an injunction prohibiting Thomas from making sound recordings available for distribution. Graduate student Joel Tenenbaum found himself in a similar position with jury-determined damages of $675,000 for the downloading of thirty-one songs owned by Sony BMG Music Entertainment. Ironically, according to an anonymous email to Harvard law professor George Nesson, who was assisting Tenenbaum in his legal battle, thirty out of the thirty-one songs in question were available for free download via the Chinese website for Google Music (Anonymous 2011). Despite the crippling financial burden of such cases, the lawsuits did not appear to deter file sharers: the American Assembly at Columbia University reported that 46 per cent of adults (those over 30) and 70 per cent of 18- to 29-year-olds have "bought, copied or downloaded unauthorized music, TV shows or movies" (Karaganis 2011: 2).

A Post-Walkman World

While the recording industry was busy suing its fans, it was also experimenting with attempts to monetize digital audio and convert some file sharers into paying customers. In its early days, the poor quality and lack of portability of MP3s compared to CDs made it difficult to build a business model around digital music. Copyright issues also played a big factor, resulting in various proprietary formats, players and devices.

Early attempts by the major labels to sell digital music were largely unsuccessful. Label-controlled services such as Sony and Universal's Pressplay and Warner, EMI and BMG's MusicNet (Gordon 2005: 89) received a lot of criticism for their complicated licensing system and lack of artists. PC World placed Pressplay at number nine in its 2007 roll call of the twenty-five worst tech products of all time; its "stunningly brain-dead features showed that the record companies still didn't get it" (Tynan 2006). Given the large margins that it made on the CD format, the industry was reluctant to pursue selling songs online, despite the scale of file-sharing networks and the increasing sales of portable mp3 players, which indicated that there was potentially a massive demand for digital audio files. Many saw this failure to engage as a short-sighted error of judgement.

In 2009, musician John Mellencamp lambasted the recording industry for not knowing how to handle the new trajectory that music appeared to be following. He wrote,

> [T]echnology, just as it always does, progressed. That which, by all rights, should have had a positive impact for all of us – better sound quality, accessibility, and portability – is now being blamed for many of the ills that beset the music business. The captains of the industry, it seemed, proved themselves incapable of having a broader, more long-range view of what this new technology offered. The music business is very complicated in itself so it's understandable that these additional elements were not dealt with coherently in light of the distractions that abound. Not understanding the possibilities, they ignorantly turned it into a nightmarish situation. The nightmare is the fact that they simply didn't know how to make it work for us. (Mellencamp 2009)

But others did understand the potential and were working to build a future for commercialized recorded music initially centred on the MP3 format. Whilst the music industry had been an integral part of the development of earlier music formats such as the vinyl LP and the CD, the MP3 format had evolved from outside the industry – as part of a rapidly developing personal computer marketplace. In its early days, MP3 playback was restricted to that personal computer, but stand-alone players inevitably emerged – again, from sources external to the traditional music industries.

In 1998 SaeHan Information Systems released the MPMan F10. The MPMan could hold only 32MB of data, good for about ten songs at 64kbps (about a fifth of CD quality). Whilst it was not well received, its successor

– the Diamond Rio PMP300 – gained the attention of consumers and the recording industry. The Rio cost around US$200, boasted a host of features including EQ and an LCD screen and came with Music Match, music library software. It is worth noting that Diamond Multimedia, the manufacturer of the Rio, had established itself as a producer of integrated personal computer peripherals such as graphics and sound cards. The extension of its product line to portable music players predicted the involvement of the computer industries in the future of music.

Though failing to see the bigger opportunities, the recording industry appeared to be able to distinguish a clear threat. In 1998 the RIAA realized the potential impact of MP3 if it was allowed to run amok and outside its influence. It attempted to block sales of the Rio, alleging that the device did "not meet the requirements for digital audio recording devices under the Audio Home Recording Act of 1992" because it did "not employ a Serial Copyright Management System" (*Recording Industry Association of America* v. *Diamond Multimedia System* [1999]).

Unfortunately for the RIAA, the case was unsuccessful – the pivotal point in the judgment concerned the nature of digital audio and cultural uses for a computer. In order to be a "digital audio recording device" under the Act, the Rio had to be capable of reproducing a "digital music recording" either "directly" or "from a transmission". The court determined that the computer hard drive responsible for uploading MP3s to the Rio was not a digital music recording because it contained much more than "only sounds, and material, statements, or instruction incidental to those fixed sounds". The rapid shift of media to digital data placed the computer and the Rio outside the scope of the Act.

Further, the court noted that the Rio's purpose aligned with the primary purpose of the Act, "the facilitation of personal use" by "merely making copies in order to render portable, or 'space shift', those files that already reside on a user's hard drive". After losing this case, the RIAA shifted its attention away from manufacturers of MP3 players to one of the primary sources of MP3s – file-sharing networks in general, and Napster in particular. Diamond went on to sell 200,000 Rios: significant early sales, but a drop in the ocean compared to what was to come.

The introduction of Apple's iPod in 2001 marked the beginning of the mainstreaming of digital music players. It met with a relatively muted reception from the largely techie consumer group that had until then been the main market for mp3 players. (A famous Slashdot post from "CmdrTaco" commented: "No wireless. Less space than a Nomad. Lame" [CmdrTaco 2001].) But Apple had managed to create a convenient and easy-to-use device that would evolve into a complete multimedia ecosystem and by October 2011 it had sold over 300 million iPods (Albanesius 2011).

At the time of the iPod's introduction, the MP3 format threatened the recording industry's control over music distribution. It also threatened the industry's relevance for artists emerging into a culture of distributed networking. For record labels, the digital music arena was in chaos. File-sharing networks were distributing copyrighted files left, right and centre. Label-controlled business initiatives were providing inadequate and the industry floundered in its attempts to find a satisfactory solution. It was clear that the industry needed a white knight, but really had no idea where to look for one.

As it turned out, the industry's salvation was a computer company – and one which has since manoeuvred itself into a controlling role in the music business. As Apple's iPod digital music players were becoming dominant, it was clear that providing a source for musical content would be a critical next step. Steven Levy's *The Perfect Thing* (2006) describes Apple's moves into the music industry, noting that the company had difficulty convincing major labels to provide content for what would become the iTunes Music Store. The majors were still of the mind that any foray into digital downloads would further damage their existing markets and exacerbate what they saw as widespread piracy. Apple's CEO, Steve Jobs, targeted Doug Morris first, knowing that if he managed to gain the confidence of Universal then the other majors would surely follow (Levy 2006: 158). According to Levy, the swaying factor was Apple's limited share of the personal computer market: iTunes would only be available to Macintosh users, which at the time of the store's launch in 2003 comprised about 5 per cent of the market. The store rounded out Apple's digital music ecosystem – its successful iPod music players being the other key component of the strategy.

The serious caveat of the labels' involvement with iTunes was their demand for digital rights management (DRM) to prevent their digital offerings slipping into the shadow economy of free music exchange. Mnookin (2007) astutely notes that Steve Jobs managed to turn the DRM mandate into a bonus for his business and locked in the retail end of the online market. Despite the limitations forced onto digital music formats, the iPod and iPhone family has proven an unbridled success. By initially rendering songs purchased through the iTunes stores incompatible with any other media player, Apple acquired its stranglehold on the market for digital music. iTunes went live in 2003 with 200,000 songs on offer and six months later was offered to Windows users. Over time, its catalogue of music expanded dramatically, and it became clear that there was a legitimate market for legal digital music.

By 2010, iTunes had sold its ten-billionth song. The store has been a mixed blessing for the major labels. Rio Caraeff, Universal's executive vice-president in charge of digital strategy, said, "The problem is, [Jobs] became a gatekeeper. We make a lot of money from him, and suddenly you're wearing golden handcuffs. We would hate to give up that income" (Mnookin 2007). Computers had upset the recording industry's applecart with the invention and proliferation of the MP3 format, so it was little surprise that it took a computer company to stabilize the situation.

iTunes was never alone in the market, although its competitors may not have been as successful, something arguably attributable to Apple's double-pronged approach in marketing not just music, but something to play it on. The current music catalogues of iTunes and its competitors are wholly free of digital rights management, allowing for interoperability between devices. The last decade has seen the emergence of a number of new intermediaries, of which iTunes is but one. These will be explored in greater detail in the following chapter.

Digital music sales, though, have undoubtedly grown. According to the RIAA's statistics, in 2004 CD sales accounted for 92.7 per cent of the total market, with digital revenue (singles and albums) making up a sliver at just 1.5 per cent. By 2010 the picture had changed dramatically; CDs accounted for just 49.1 per cent whereas digital revenue (expanded to include subscriptions, mobile and music videos) constituted 43.3 per cent of the US recording industry's total income. The RIAA's 2012 figures indicate further growth with the digital market comprising 59 per cent of total sales, a factor largely attributed to "access models" such as Spotify and Rhapsody. Similarly, the British Phonographic Industry (BPI) reported that the digital market was healthily growing. Geoff Taylor, the BPI's chief executive, stated that 2011 was "another record year for digital singles, but the most encouraging news of the year is the strong backing consumers are giving to the digital album format" (BPI 2012: 1). As encouraging as this growth is, Taylor reinforces the industry's continued investment in physical media: "Digital developments grab the headlines, but the CD remains hugely popular with consumers, accounting for three-quarters of album sales. Physical ownership is important to many fans and the CD will be a key element of the market for years to come." His predictions were proved correct when the 2012 statistics revealed that the CD still accounted for 69.1 per cent of album sales, whilst sales of digital albums rose by 14.8 per cent.

Despite this newfound legitimacy, what the industry calls piracy is still rampant across peer-to-peer networks, torrents, swarms and digital lockers such as Putlocker and Rapidshare, and the fights against it continue with the high-profile case against Kim Dotcom of Mega (and formerly MegaUpload) and controversial, yet ultimately stymied, proposals for US legislation such as Stop Online Piracy Act and Protect IP Act. Whilst the piracy situation is deemed serious enough to consider "breaking the internet", it remains important not to allow the more spurious online activities to overshadow the boons which the networked environment has granted to musicians worldwide. The same technologies used to redistribute copyrighted works without permission are also used, along with numerous and diverse legal services, by amateur and independent musicians to distribute their own original works without a record label.

Perhaps most importantly, the digital music scene initially emerged without the music industry's involvement. The industry has traditionally been in control of its new media forms every step of the way through either direct development or intimate partnerships. The social energy of MP3, however, escaped the industry's notice until it was too late. But the initial dust of *this* music revolution appears to have largely settled. New business models and music services appear and disappear with regularity. Labels, artists and fans are exploiting the full power of the web and the network environment. Debates over cloud music (where music files are stored on a remote server and streamed via the internet rather than being downloaded to the user's computer) ensue. The ways in which music is produced, discovered, acquired, consumed and shared have once again been irrevocably changed and appear to keep changing. The dominion of the record label has been diminished – its rise and potential fall will be further examined in the next two chapters.

4 The New Intermediaries

In January 1954, a young truck driver walked into the Memphis Recording Service during his lunch break and recorded a song to give to his mother. The Service was run by Sam Phillips and, as well as recording music for weddings and parties and personal tributes, it released songs under the Sun Records label. Phillips heard the truck driver's recording, invited him to record other songs, and the career of one Elvis Presley was born. Presley signed with Sun and released five singles, but he needed the clout of a major record company and so he moved to RCA Victor when his contract expired. The rest is history.

The role of people like Phillips, and manager Tom Parker, as well as the networks of influence of companies such as RCA Victor, were instrumental in the success of artists like Elvis Presley. As intermediaries, their access to recording studios, radio stations and the live music industry was essential in gaining the exposure required to make and sell records. For most of the twentieth century, the pathway to musical success was to get a recording contract – to sign with an intermediary record label that had the experience and influence to enable an individual to establish a career in music.

In the last chapter, we saw that the new media technologies offered new possibilities for musicians. Web 2.0, underpinned by the networked connection of powerful multimedia computing devices, has seen a move towards disintermediation. Many commercial transactions now eliminate the so-called middleman. For example, the personal computer space is replete with manufacturers like Dell and Apple selling directly to the public or to other businesses. Similarly, online retailers in sectors ranging from clothing (Lands' End, Levi's, Nike) to cars (Subaru in Australia) sell directly to customers, bypassing shop fronts. In the media space, high-profile bloggers and tweeps (Twitter users who follow each other across numerous social media platforms) no longer require the brand of a newspaper or magazine to communicate with their readers. And in the realm of music, the rise of accessible recording technologies and online distribution is a combination which has allowed musicians to sell their music direct to their audiences without involving the usual chain of intermediaries – record labels, publishers, distributors, wholesalers and retailers.

But the apparent disintermediation is by no means absolute. Retail aggregators continue, as do media companies and record labels, although they face new competition. As well as potential disintermediation, the new technologies with their lower barriers to entry have enabled new intermediaries to emerge, challenging the previously dominant players. So eBay and Amazon threaten the old department stores, Gawker and Huffington Post aggregate blogs and challenge the older media companies and a range of new music intermediaries provides new opportunities for musicians and audiences.

Like most technological and social changes, disintermediation has its boosters and dissenters. In the previous chapter we saw how Stefan Heller, CEO of Peoplesound.com, had predicted that disintermediation was the key to the future and traditional record labels were on the brink of extinction. The last decade has proven the hyperbolic nature of Heller's claims. Of course, record labels are still with us, but that does not mean that nothing has changed. The number of musicians engaging directly with their audiences suggests that disintermediation has occurred – just not to the extent that some had predicted. Moreover, the confluence of the network and the personal computer has led to not only disintermediation but also reintermediation, to sit alongside traditional business models. As Michael Carroll (2006: 45) notes,

> After the revolutionary euphoria died down ... many acknowledged that intermediaries are necessary to all kinds of transactions in commerce, culture, and news. Reintermediation soon follows from disintermediation, and the real question the internet posed was not whether intermediaries are necessary but *what kinds* of intermediaries are necessary.

Certainly, the established recording industry has been rocked by a plethora of events that took music in a trajectory that was not predicted, much less prepared for, but as the initial dust settled a retail market for (authorized) digital music emerged – and the established players of the recording industry are not its sole occupants.

The current music industry ecology is complex; a swarm of traditional, new and hybrid business models and approaches stem from an array of entities so interrelated it is sometimes difficult to draw any real lines of division. Major and independent labels continue to issue hardcopy media formats as well as digital releases via numerous new intermediaries (iTunes and Amazon, and smaller, specialist retailers such as Beatport or Juno) whilst leveraging fan bases through social media networks. These same approaches are available to individual artists (independents and those previously signed with recording labels), who may also employ the services of aggregators like TuneCore to manage the distribution of releases to online retailers or CD Baby (which also offers CD sales).

The recording industry and musicians are currently negotiating a bridge between a twentieth-century business model based on selling a physical artefact and a plethora of new models that cohabit a new, networked music ecosystem. And they are negotiating it during a period where audiences – and musicians – are reshaping their habits and practices. But the dynamic between musician and audience has changed; the old ways remain, but there are now many ways for music to be distributed and consumed for profit and for free, legitimately and otherwise. Some methods are used to directly generate income, and others are used for more promotional purposes.

Music analyst Mark Mulligan (2011) reflects,

> I am of the age group that grew up with CDs. I am part of the transition generation that has enthusiastically adopted digital but still understands the value of physical media and ownership. The Digital Natives however (i.e. those consumers who have grown up in the digital age without ever having learned the habit of buying physical media) have entirely different concepts of ownership.

The culture of Mulligan's Digital Natives is focused on access rather than ownership, since they are time-rich and cash-poor. In this context, it is unsurprising that services such as Spotify and YouTube are so popular. *The Economist* in 2008 wrote of an apocryphal 2006 focus-group session where EMI (then the world's fourth biggest record label) invited a group of teenagers to London to discuss their listening habits, with the hope of determining "what the kids wanted" from record labels in the twenty-first century. As a thank-you, the teens were told to help themselves to a big pile of CDs. Although they were free, none of the teenagers took any of the CDs. It is important, however, not to overstate the uptake of purely digital music. Much fan activity still revolves around twentieth-century practices; for such fans "you either buy music and own it, or you listen to it on the radio or TV. Their worldview remains wholly un-muddied by cloud and streaming services" (Mulligan 2011).

This chapter is concerned with the new intermediaries that have evolved in the twenty-first-century music ecology. It explores the remediation of music through describing some of the new key and innovative players; distributors, aggregators, widgets and social media networks provide a network of possibilities that challenge established models of artist/audience engagement as well as the very value of recorded music. Providing a complete taxonomy of online intermediaries would require much more than a single chapter. Indeed, the dynamic nature of the environment in question precludes any such taxonomy being totally comprehensive. Instead, this chapter is more interested in presenting a broad overview of the layers of services emerging from the affordances of the network.

Why intermediaries?

Traditionally, artists seeking to offer their music to audiences have required intermediaries such as recording labels, distributors, retailers, touring companies, managers, publishers and radio stations. Each link in the supply chain offers services beyond the reach of the individual artist. For example, before the internet and affordable computer-based home studios, recording labels were necessary to provide the capital required to record an album of sufficient quality to meet the demands of audiences. Airplay by radio stations was – and to a great extent still is – considered a crucial ingredient in launching a band or artist. Radio play promotes music and drives consumer interest towards record sales and live performances; and, of course, affiliation with a label was the key to accessing precious radio time. The narrow strip of opportunities placed these forms of intermediaries in the role of gatekeepers between musician and audience.

Naturally, during the label-dominated era of music production and distribution there have been the exceptions where an artist's success has seemingly occurred outside traditional channels. For example, the John Butler Trio enjoyed a debut at number 1 in the ARIA charts with *Sunrise Over Sea* (2004), an album released by MGM Distribution, the largest independent record distributor in Australia. Not to play down Butler's success, but his approach was still predicated on the same production model used by the major labels – the marketing and sale of a recorded artefact, a process involving many of the traditionally required intermediaries. Perhaps more truly independent success was demonstrated by Jimmy Cauty and Bill Drummond (aka the Justified Ancients of Mu Mu, the Timelords and the KLF), whose various hits were released via their own label – KLF Communications – and distributed in the UK by a cooperative network of independent distributors known as "The Cartel". Again, not to downplay Cauty and Drummond's success, but their distribution in the USA was handled by Arista, a (now defunct and absorbed in RCA Records) subsidiary of Sony Music Entertainment. Arguably, Cauty and Drummond would not have enjoyed popularity in the USA without the involvement of a major intermediary like Arista.

The digital shift has added scores of new players to the music ecology. The opening of the floodgates between artists and audiences has not only exposed a wealth of new talent but also necessitated new gatekeepers, online distributors and aggregators on whom we rely to filter and service our general and specific needs; some, such as Beatport and Juno Records have specialized, whilst others like iTunes, Amazon and Spotify pursue a more generalist path.

Beyond any initial production costs (e.g., software, studio time, mastering), the retail overheads in selling digital music files are significantly reduced compared to selling their physical counterpart. Kevin Kelly (2007) notes,

> Over time the cost per fixed technological function will decrease. If that function persists long enough its costs begin to approach (but never reach) zero. In the goodness of time any particular technological function will exist as if it were free.

Further, the equalizing effect allows for unsigned artists to sell their music side by side with the biggest names from both the present day and yesteryear. This apparent democratization of music, however, is not quite as idyllic as its technical possibilities might suggest. The ideal of directly connecting artists and audiences (willing to pay for music) is subject to qualification.

The potential for disintermediated success is enhanced by an already present public profile and established fan bases. For bands like Nine Inch Nails, alternative delivery and active engagement have become deeply entrenched in the artist/fan relationship. The household-name status enjoyed by Radiohead – one predominantly built via the twentieth-century model – made it easier to sell *In Rainbows* (2007) directly to fans. Saul Williams's third album *The Inevitable Rise And Liberation Of Niggy Tardust!* (2007) was released via NiggyTardust.com for fans to download for free or they could pay $5 for better-quality versions of the songs. Whilst Williams does not enjoy the high profile of NIN or Radiohead, his album was produced and publicized by Trent Reznor, an endorsement that carries more than a modicum of cultural currency.

Those interesting examples of disintermediation do exist, but they are hardly reflective of the wider music community that uses the network to gain exposure. Radiohead's Thom Yorke distances the release of *In Rainbows* from any notion of an emergent business model:

> The only reason we could even get away with this, the only reason anyone even gives a shit, is the fact that we've gone through the whole mill of the business in the first place. It's not supposed to be a model for anything else. It was simply a response to a situation. We're out of contract. We have our own studio. We have this new server. What the hell else would we do? This was the obvious thing. But it only works for us because of where we are. (Byrne and Yorke 2007)

For the present authors, the most compelling characteristics of Music 2.0 are the unprecedented opportunities for independent musicians – those trying to carve out a living without label involvement. Few artists enjoy fan bases on the scale of Radiohead and NIN. However, for many having a large fan base is a problem that has never existed: many artists would not have an audience at all if not for the web. Others have used the web to expand a scope limited by time, money, ambition or appeal. There are no hard-and-fast rules, simply opportunities, and this is what makes this aspect of Music 2.0 difficult to document. The new media have provided many opportunities for artists to connect directly with audiences and to monetize creativity in the form of recorded-music sales, live performances and merchandise. By leveraging the new technologies, artists are able to craft careers that look very different from traditional pathways.

Contrary to utopian ideas about disintermediation, the evolution of the digital music ecology has demonstrated that the new intermediaries are a must for the unsigned or independent artist hoping to sell music. Certainly, a musician seeking to monetize his/her music is not obligated to use an online distributor. A personal website and a PayPal account may serve as a business infrastructure, but the visibility of major online distributors underlines their usefulness. Apple's iTunes store is now the number one music retailer in the world, and, along with other major online outlets such as Amazon, it dominates online music sales. Similarly, in smaller niche markets, there are dominant players.

For example, according to Joseph Stopps, who runs Dtox Records, Beatport (specializing in electronic dance music) controls an estimated 80 to 90 per cent of the electronic music online market (McManus 2010) and in February 2011 it struck a licensing deal with EMI to distribute its dance catalogue across the USA, Europe and Australia. EMI's dance roster includes Depeche Mode, Kylie Minogue, Daft Punk and Gorillaz (Peoples 2011).

John Alderman (2001) does an excellent job of providing a history of digital music communities and industries. Tracking the emergence and uptake of digital formats across a range of networked scenarios, he portrays the birth and challenging early years of digital music. When Alderman was writing *Sonic Boom*, online distribution was still relatively immature (and dare we say naïve). A lot has happened since then. MySpace emerged as *the* place to be for music until its user base shifted allegiance to Facebook. As more legitimate online retailers have emerged, more fans are willing to pay for music and purely digital music is heading towards becoming the default. In 2012 the International Federation of the Phonographic Industry, which represents the recording industry worldwide, reported for the first time that

> Digital channels have overtaken physical formats to become the dominant revenue stream in the world's largest market, the U.S. And the digital music market is poised to further expand its reach internationally in 2012. (IFPI 2012)

As this transition occurs, new intermediaries continue to step in to manage the transactions, discoveries and sharing of music.

Selling Music

Digital music offers many advantages over physical media. An iPod simply offers more portability for music (as well as other media) than a Walkman or a Discman. Today the relative storage capabilities are incomparable; no longer is there a need for large pockets to hold extra cassettes or CDs. Additionally – and DRM aside – the ease of transferring, sharing, copying and/or burning digital music facilitates movement between devices and between fans. For the entrepreneurial artist, digital music provides a highly efficient and cost-effective solution to distribution. The master track can be duplicated time and time again with no loss of quality (unless imposed by format compression) and with no cost to the artist. A single recording can be uploaded to any number of online distribution sites and gain exposure to millions of potential fans. This is the promise of democratized music, but the reality involves navigating licence agreements, terms and conditions and understanding royalty payments, Universal Product and International Standard Recording Codes, amongst other factors, many of which may appear esoteric to the uninitiated.

The range of outlets through which an artist can sell music is imposing. Beyond the obvious iTunes and Amazon, there exists an extended landscape populated by a range of services and specializations. Yet even the major new intermediaries require work. The gates to the iTunes store are tightly regulated by a hierarchical system. All but the most prolific of artists are immediately excluded from directly approaching iTunes; applicants are required to have at least twenty albums in their catalogue and a US tax ID. Apple's strong position in the music economy allows it to delegate the acquisition of product to a second tier of online distributors and aggregators – the company provides a list of recommended aggregators, but it is far from exhaustive (Apple 2011).

In the typical financial arrangement for a song that retails for $0.99, Apple keeps $0.34 and the remainder goes to the distributor, who may be a label, online distributor or an artist. For reasons already pointed out, it is atypical for an artist to deal directly with iTunes. An intermediary such as a record label or online distributor usually provides the link between artist and outlet. Many distributors offer aggregation services whereby they will sell your music via their own site and others, including those at the top tier. Naturally, these services either exact payment from the sale itself or charge a fee for facilitating the distribution of the song. There are far too many to discuss individually, so we will focus on some of the key players.

CD Baby was started by Derek Sivers in 1997 but sold in 2008 to Disc Makers for $22 million as part of a philanthropic venture; Sivers used the money to establish a charitable trust providing music education. CD Baby's philosophy is simple: "a company run BY musicians FOR musicians ... No distributors. No major labels. We only sell music that musicians send us directly." In March 2013 CD Baby boasted nearly 400,000 individual albums and over three million digital tracks. Signing up with CD Baby was easy, but some costs were involved. There was a one-time set-up fee of US$39 per album or $9.99 per single. If CD Baby was selling CDs on behalf of the artist, the latter had to supply the stock, a minimum of five copies, but was able to set the price. CD Baby took $4 per sale, no matter what the price; CDs that sold for $15 gave the artist $11. Whilst the intermediaries of the networked music economy can provide artists with hard cash, CD Baby also provides information about the consumer (an opt-in policy). This provides artists with the opportunity to forge direct connections and value-added relationships with fans. CD Baby's digital arrangements are similarly fair. For 9% of each transaction it will

> quickly get you up for sale with all the big guys like iTunes (in 48 hours), Amazon MP3, Rhapsody, Napster, and eMusic, the interesting guys like MOG, the new guys (Spotify), mobile guys (Verizon), and many more.

For the artist, there is little to do; once the music has been supplied, CD Baby handles everything else.

Founded in 2005, TuneCore distributes music to the largest online retailers – iTunes, Amazon, Rhapsody, eMusic and Spotify. Whilst CD Baby has emerged as a champion of independent artists, TuneCore promotes itself as the choice for the cutting-edge independent musician: "Use TuneCore to get your music everywhere" states Nine Inch Nails' Trent Reznor on the site's home page. What better endorsement than from the band that outspokenly rejected record labels in favour of artist-entrepreneurship? Similarly, guitar virtuoso Steve Vai's testament reads, "In the most unequivocally depressing time in the music business, TuneCore reinvents the wheel, and it's not even round anymore." Unlike CD Baby, TuneCore charges annual fees for managing songs, $9.99 per single and ringtone and $49.99 per album, but passes all proceeds onto the artist.

Music and the web have fitted together like hand and glove. There is so much music available online from the plethora of online distributors, official and personal websites, video-sharing and social network sites, blogs, and music magazines, as well as more shady distribution locales. It is difficult to even estimate the sheer volume, hence the requirement for filtering mechanisms. Artists signed to labels have an obvious advantage when it comes to promotion as they are able to tap into the new media opportunities as well as the traditional offline avenues for promotion. For the independent artist, however, standing out in the crowd is much more challenging. Distributors such as CD Baby and TuneCore provide many opportunities for independent artists – opportunities, lest we forget, that did not exist a decade ago. The artist gains access to the financial side of the music economy, but there is still a lot of work to be done in the attention economy. Few (hopefully) are naïve enough to believe that one simply produces and uploads a track before sitting back to watch the money flow in. In many ways, the solutions provided by online distributors are the easier part of the equation.

Selling Free

One of the biggest challenges faced by independent artists is gaining exposure to audiences. The internet provides a number of opportunities for artists to introduce their music to new audiences. The access barriers that once stood between producer and audience have been lowered, and in some cases completely eliminated. Cost, equipment, infrastructure and time have all been drastically affected by the digital shift. The costs involved in setting up a broadcast radio station prohibit most private individuals from doing so. Internet radio stations and podcasts, by way of contrast, provide a low-cost entry into this arena. The multitude of internet radio stations can be divided into two categories. First, there are those affiliated with traditional broadcast radio stations. The broadcast content is frequently offered via streaming audio or as downloadable podcasts. Second, there are independent internet-only radio stations. Like their mainstream counterparts, content is streamed or downloaded via the network using websites, widgets, apps, and music players such as Winamp or iTunes. Due to the costs involved in licensing label music, many internet-only stations draw from the wealth of independently produced music found online. As with broadcast radio, internet-only radio spans every genre imaginable (and some that may surprise you). Internet-only radio stations provide independent artists with an opportunity to attract individuals into seeking out more of their music. Of course, the success of this strategy is restricted by several factors, not the least of which is the size of the radio station's audience. The uncertainty, however, is offset by the relative ease of achieving internet radio play. The submission process typically involves simply emailing the producer an mp3, a brief bio and further contact details.

Unencumbered by rights management protocols, digital music is easily shared through a diverse range of mechanisms in addition to those already mentioned. Sharing, however, can take up a lot of time. For example, an artist wishing to distribute music via MySpace, Facebook, Bandcamp and his or her own website is forced to laboriously upload copies of songs to each platform. This is where new players such as SoundCloud are useful by providing a centralized repository and an embeddable widget.

Sound designers Alex Ljung and Eric Wahlforss started SoundCloud in 2007 with the intention of producing a system whereby musicians could share recordings with one another, but this vision expanded into a means of distribution. SoundCloud makes sharing its central feature. Its utility stems from the widgets used to distribute and promote music rather than just the artist. Whilst embedding a "free website mp3 player" is easy for the tech savvy, the artist must have write access to the website. In addition to websites or blogs, the social networking leviathans Facebook and Twitter support SoundCloud's widgets, thus enabling artists to greatly extend their reach across a range of platforms. Additionally, SoundCloud's Application Programming Interface (API) is available for smartphone developers wishing to integrate music into iPhone and Android apps. The value of SoundCloud lies in the ease with which it can be implemented across multiple platforms. In many ways, SoundCloud does for music what YouTube does for video.

In *New Music Strategies: The 20 Things You Must Know about Music Online* Andrew Dubber advises

> By far the most reliable way to promote music is to have people hear it. Repeatedly, if possible – and for free. After a while, if you're lucky, people get to know and love the music. Sooner or later, they're going to want to own it ... That's the order it has to happen in. It can't happen in any other order. There's no point in hoping that people will buy the music, then hear it, then like it. They just won't. (2007: 14)

Radio has proved this. For fans to buy music they must develop some relationship with the song and/or the artist. Established artists have an obvious advantage when selling music online. They already have fans looking for their products. For the independent artists, things are not so easy.

Radio was – and for many artists, remains – the primary tool for promoting music. Whilst community stations may offer some airplay to independent artists, the major stations typically remain bound in historical relationships with the major labels. The network, however, has opened up other possibilities for promoting music.

In 2006 the authors surveyed and interviewed a number of Australian musicians. Respondents hailed from diverse corners of the music industries; bedroom amateurs to professional DJs, pub bands to those with Top Ten success. From the responses two things were immediately obvious. First, most artists were at least aware of, if not engaged in a growing dependence on, MySpace, which in 2006 was *l'enfant terrible* of the web 2.0 platform. Characterized by anarchic user profiles, for bands it was *the* place to be. MySpace quickly established itself as a key place to promote music and build relationships with fans. In the sea of profiles, established, independent and amateur artists "friended" each other, updated gig information, shared photos, audio and video, and commented on each other's work. Second, many of the interviewees were disparaging of the traditional recording industry. For some, this attitude stemmed from mistrust of an industry desperately trying to control music through suing fans and DRM (as was the way at the time). Others, however, were fully cognizant of the possibilities of Music 2.0 for managing their own musical destinies and had no desire to sign with a label.

MySpace's heyday is well behind it now, but the potentials of the networked environment remain and have developed further. To catalogue the full gamut of services available to independent musicians would take an encyclopaedia. But, in truth, the most interesting aspects of these new services and technologies are how they are *used*. In addition to the online distributors covered above, there is a range of services that can variously impact on an artist's career. Much has changed in the years since our survey of Australian musicians. Considered important enough to be the subject of a major motion picture and boasting in excess of a billion users, with a level of activity far outstripping MySpace's best efforts, Facebook requires little introduction. Zuckerberg's social network is predicated on sharing. The ease of promoting and sharing music via Facebook – using a band profile, the platform's native music-player applications and/or embedding widgets offered by services such as SoundCloud – means there is a previously unimaginable spectrum of opportunities for independent artists.

In September 2011, Facebook announced partnerships with sixteen music services including Spotify, MOG, Rhapsody, SoundCloud and Rdio. At the most trivial level, Facebook's integration with supported music services allows fans to announce to their friends what they are listening to and for those friends to hear those same songs. Facebook's approach to music is markedly different from that of iTunes, Amazon or TuneCore, which all focus on selling recorded music. By contrast, Facebook integrates a number of social media services and primarily concentrates on sharing. Sharing here, however, is different from peer-to-peer file sharing. This is not a case of piracy but of recommendation and discovery of music via one of the most popular websites. Facebook, of course, benefits by accumulating information that indicates listening trends but without having to license a single song. It is too early to say with any certainty, but by virtue of its position in social networking, Facebook appears to stand on the brink of being one of the new leading intermediaries of music. By highlighting and cataloguing previously hidden listening trends, the socialization of music has the potential to once more reconfigure how we might engage with music. Facebook may well not be the leading light of social networking forever, but in 2012 its collaboration with various music services is indicative of the convergent currents sweeping across the recording industry.

Talk of global networks, connectivity and sharing again risks a hyperbolic portrayal of the future directions of music. It is worth remembering that streaming music services do not comfortably fit with many fans' consumption practices – which are predicated on owning, if not a physical object, then its virtual facsimile. Additionally, in the global connected network, it is easy to forget the national borders that can be reinforced through technology (or lack thereof). For example, Australia did not receive Spotify until 2012, much to the chagrin of the present authors, who had to content themselves with reading about the service, rather than enjoying the first-hand experience.

The development of smartphone technologies and markets has facilitated a further intersection as online platforms, personal relationships and mobile networks converge. Web-based content can be accessed via smartphones, but the mobile platform offers artists new opportunities to engage with fans. For example, the free-to-download NIN Access iPhone app provides Nine Inch Nails fans with a unique experience. In addition to displaying the official Twitter feed and latest news, the app provides access to a variety of audio-visual media, including the entire NIN discography. There is a strong community aspect to the app with messaging, forums and a location-based shoutbox (a feature that allows website users to quickly leave – or "shout" – a message to other users). All content is centralized online so that the app can be easily updated. Further, the reach of the NIN fan community stems outward from the website to the mobile networks.

Whilst the intersection of networks produces numerous combinations of opportunities for artists, there are some hurdles. Some solutions require technical knowledge of the web. For example, in setting up an independent website, an artist must secure a domain name and then host as well as build the site, navigating HTML, CSS, JavaScript and possibly PHP and trying to integrate third-party elements such as Twitter widgets, music players, shopping carts and PayPal systems. Programming an iPhone or Android app requires a knowledge of programming languages far more challenging than any mentioned in connection with the website. For some artists this is a viable option. There is nothing to say that a computer programmer cannot also produce jazz music. For everyone else who is limited in the ability or time required for doing so there is the range of new Music 2.0 services. For example, Ajolive Music Network (http://ajolive.com) offered "3 of the most important tools that allow music creators to share their music on the internet: iPhone app, Facebook fan page and website/community". In addition to setting up a Facebook fan page and a website (at the time of writing, these services were "coming soon"), Ajolive offered a customized iPhone app on a monthly subscription basis. The costs may have deterred many independent artists. The minimum 12-month contract included several one-off set-up fees, resulting in a total of US$2370, excluding website design, which was quoted separately.

The huge number of online music distribution possibilities can appear daunting to the independent artist without label or management support to handle the business side of things: Should I distribute my music via a personal website with a widget allowing direct purchase or try and get it on the big retailers? Should I target boutique music outlets or try for something more general like Amazon? How do I even get my songs on Amazon? How do they promote my music once it's available for sale? What about social media? If I provide promotional streams of my music, will people actually pay to download it? How much money will I actually get from each sale on iTunes or play on Spotify? These are all genuine concerns. The network provides a myriad of distribution possibilities and just as many for remuneration.

But Wait. There's More

The web has given rise to a number of alternative models for distributing music. Arguably, the online distribution models used by Amazon, iTunes and innumerable other retailers are not a million miles away from the traditional twentieth-century model. Certainly, the access barriers that once excluded independent artists have been removed, but ultimately the practice of selling music is still largely predicated on a commodified recording, albeit intangible.

The web is more than just a set of technical affordances that enable cost-effective distribution of information in all forms across multiple platforms. As Sir Tim Berners-Lee reminds us, it is also about connecting people (Laningham 2006). Some artists have leveraged this principle to purify the practice of music.

The British rock band Marillion formed in 1979 and has released music through EMI in the UK and Capitol in the USA. In a guest blog post for *The Telegraph* (7 August 2008), Marillion's keyboard player Mark Kelly described how, after completing its business with major labels, the band decided to embark on a different approach.

> In 1999 we released our final contracted album for Castle Records and, in anticipation of the way we planned to do business in the future, called it Marillion.com. We had already collected the email

addresses of more than 20,000 fans through free CDs, downloads, etc. and by asking these fans to order and pay for the upcoming CD in advance, we were able to finance the writing and recording. We maximised the profit from the pre-order by cutting out the record companies, distributors and retailers, manufacturing and shipping direct. We also released the album in the shops through an independent distributor to reach the fans not on the internet.

We released three more albums between 2001 and 2007 using this business model and despite continuing falls in CD sales worldwide we have managed to shield ourselves from the worst by continuing to build our database of email addresses, currently more than 65,000, and by offering special edition pre-order CDs with 128-page hardcover books containing beautiful artwork. I'm sure many people still download our music illegally but the real hardcore fans want the special editions and are willing to pay £25 or more for them.

Marillion's experimentation with crowd-funded patronage may have been positive, but this approach is not for everyone. Marillion has three decades of established mainstream success behind it. That said, this example points to some of the possibilities realized through the connections afforded by the network. In *Linchpin*, Seth Godin writes, "the winners are the ... artists who *give* gifts" (2010: 238). Marillion's approach is not just about selling a commodified artefact but giving its fans the opportunity to directly contribute to its production. Nine Inch Nails takes the relationship with the audience in a slightly different direction and rewards fans with a more intimate experience. USB drives hidden in venues during the band's European tour in 2007 gifted fans with as-yet-unreleased tracks from the upcoming *Year Zero* (2007) album. Additionally, the album's release was accompanied by an alternative-reality game, clues for which were disseminated via hidden storage drives and websites.

The ability to leverage the artist/fan relationship in new ways is explored in more detail later. For now, it is enough to suggest that the new music intermediaries are varied. Certainly, there is a need for companies such as iTunes, Amazon, CD Baby and TuneCore. Whilst these new players echo twentieth-century practices, albeit on new platforms, the affordances of the network have introduced new layers of mediation such as streaming services and social networking. Crowd-funded ventures such as those described by Mark Kelly further alter traditional roles and practices by involving the audience directly in the process of production. Even newspapers are getting in on the action: Leonard Cohen exclusively pre-released *Old Ideas* (2012) via a SoundCloud widget embedded in a page of *The Guardian* online (23 January 2012).

We noted at the start of this chapter that the current musical ecosystem is complex and diverse, and what works for one artist may not be appropriate for others. Several key points emerge, however. First, the opportunities that have emerged for music distribution can benefit professional and amateur artists alike by displacing many of the once-essential links in the chain of supply and demand. Second, because of the opportunities for music that was once hidden to gain exposure, arguably the expectations of, and definition of, "success" are being reconfigured. Third, new forms of mediation are reshaping traditional roles. For example, fans can become distributors and financiers, and social-networking tools can turn the act of listening into promotion and publicity.

5   Star Wars

In 2000 Hilary Rosen in her capacity as CEO of the RIAA testified to Congress that "[record labels] don't create the heart and the passion of the artist, nor transform their music into reality. Their sphere of expertise is really the marketplace. It is marketing, promotion and creating the demand. Find the fans, sell the music" (US Congress. House. Committee on the Judiciary, 2000a: 120).

The media culture of the twentieth century was predominantly one which identified cultural objects that could be broadcast or sold to a mass audience. Media were created at the centre and distributed to audiences at the periphery; control was maintained by central industry players and audiences did little other than consume the material on offer. Of course, such conceptions of mass audience have long since been criticized as overly simplistic and more sophisticated understandings of audience are now more common. Audiences are reconstructed as active, engaged and far from a singular mass; Jay Rosen goes so far as to suggest a category for "the people formerly known as the audience" (2012: 13). Even before the emergence of a ubiquitous digital media network, the field of media studies has understood that audiences are engaged and active participants in the construction of meaning. Publicly responding to media products through critique, commenting and the creation of media artefacts (memes, video responses, blog posts, tweets) is now normal media practice for many, and this blurs the lines between producers and consumers, between media industry and audience. The active engagement between parties to media ecologies highlights the problems with older modes of approaching production and consumption.

This shift is seen in the everyday use of media. New ways of producing, consuming and engaging with media products are common practice; the internet has spawned products ranging from YouTube through to Amazon's Kindle ecosystem, all of which embrace new understandings of media practice. Despite (or perhaps because of) this, traditional media industries still struggle to move away from twentieth-century thinking. The television industry still relies on a relatively limited ratings methodology to determine audience numbers and advertising rates, and this approach largely overlooks emergent fora for discussion and engagement. Hollywood studios rely on blockbuster opening weekends to maintain momentum. And the music industry continues to embrace an approach that is based on creating stars and privileging chart placement as a measure of success. What's more, this approach has its roots in the technologies of a hundred years ago – an industrialized construction of stars who could be marketed in the same way as other consumer goods.

Back to the Future?

Roy Shuker defines the media phenomena of stars as "individuals who, as a consequence of their public performances or appearances in the mass media, become widely recognized and acquire symbolic status" (1998: 282). Stars are fetishized (O'Sullivan *et al.* 1994: 207; Hesmondhalgh 2006: 247), functioning as receptacles for fans' escapism from everyday life, but "stars must also be seen as economic entities, who are used to mobilize audiences and promote the products of the music industry" (Shuker 1998: 283). So, we must recognize that stars are as much a commodity as the works they produce. They are brands, attached to media objects like music albums, movies, gossip magazines and cookbooks. And it is not just media or music which is sold – musicians endorse a range of products from clothing to cars, and a roll of artists including Lady Gaga, Beyoncé and Katy Perry even lend their brand image to fragrances. The management of the star's brand is as important as the creative works attached to his or her name and properly organized can continue to generate money long after the star has ceased to perform, or has even died. For example, Elvis Presley continues to generate substantial sums of money posthumously – in 2006 the King's estate generated US$49 million (Wikström 2009: 132).

The movies and music were the incubators of the twentieth-century star system. Hollywood created movie stars and in music the seeds of the contemporary star system were planted by the phonograph companies of the early twentieth century; these companies recorded established concert musicians, capitalizing on their success to drive sales for newly emerging devices for reproducing sound. This approach was furthered with the emergence of radio in the 1920s, which "broadened the demographic base for popular music and created a huge audience for individual performers such as Eddie Cantor and Rudy Vallee, who were followed by figures such as Bing Crosby and Frank Sinatra" (Buckley and Shepherd 2003: 366). The star system became the dominant model for driving sales. David Buxton argues that music and movie stars were a necessary part of the rise of a consumerist middle class and they defined a mass culture that was designed to ensure that consumers consumed, thus enabling market-based capitalism to survive. He argues,

> Monopoly capitalism needed to increase its consumers, markets had to grow horizontally (nationally), vertically (into the working classes), and ideologically (enhanced use values) Of course this was not an automatic process. While capitalism could discipline people in work, it could not make them consume ... The rock star as a lifestyle model was the outcome of a long process that corresponded to the rise in the 1960s of a large, affluent middle class in the West. (Buxton 1983: 369)

Although initially seen as a competitive threat to the phonograph, radio emerged as the most complementary of tools and cross-media promotion of artists became common. Frith (2006: 235) notes,

> In the 1930s the recording star system depended on a tie-up with film and radio ... radio mattered most of all. By the end of the 1930s it was the most important musical medium: radio gave record companies a means of promoting their stars, while the record companies provided radio with its cheapest form of programming.

The relationship between the two industries was nothing short of symbiotic, but for the recording industry "airplay is a major determinant of sales"; as Jacob Slichter says, "There is no better guarantor of a band's success than a hit single on the radio luring listeners into record stores to buy the album" (Rossman 2012: 23).

It was clear to record company executives that radio could provide the initial exposure required by stars without any prior or concurrent presence on stage or screen. Up until this point, the recording industry had relied on horizontal integration with the arenas of performance and publishing to broker its stars, but its new relationships with radio presented new opportunities that disrupted the traditional formula.

> Companies became less concerned to exploit big stage names, more interested in building stars from scratch, as recording stars. They become less concerned to service an existing public taste than to create new tastes, to manipulate demand. (Frith 2006: 235)

This new trajectory for the recording industry marked a shift in the balance of power between the stakeholders of the early music industries. The economic emphasis shifted away from Tin Pan Alley's publishing regime towards branding record stars promoted through broadcast networks and Hollywood studios. The knock-on effect of this shift affected the practice of music itself. The determination of a "good song" was driven by its recording and marketability through the new networks of radio rather than its performative appeal in the music hall. In the 1930s, recording and broadcast platforms were tightly controlled by companies intent on creating their own stars for their own reasons – which were, naturally enough, centred on profit. It was at this stage of its evolution that the recording industry began to exemplify the characteristics indicated in Hilary Rosen's words at the beginning of this chapter: selling the right music to the right audiences in large and profitable volumes.

The story of Bing Crosby is illustrative. Crosby was an aspiring musician who moved to Los Angeles in the 1920s hoping to get a break. His vaudeville act called "Two Boys and a Piano", with his friend Al Rinker, became popular and the act evolved into a band known as the Rhythm Boys. That band released a few singles and appeared in the movie *King of Jazz* (1930). But Crosby's career took off when he landed his own radio show in 1931 – which was an enormous success, lasting thirty years and attracting millions of listeners. His star status was typical of the era. Whilst the rock-music star of the 1960s onwards was rooted in a mythology of counter-culture, Crosby was

> an archetype of what later would be described as a role model: a casual, athletic, conformist family man, who stated the 'every man who likes me sees in me the image of himself'. (Buxton 1983: 369)

The radio show coincided with Crosby's signing to a record label, leading to a string of musical hits and his elevation into perhaps the most popular singer in America and also one of its leading movie stars. Bing Crosby's rise to fame exemplifies the star-making system of the music industry: in short, identify a (talented) musician, and market him or her around a manufactured image on popular performance platforms. Although the platforms evolved over the twentieth century to encompass video and television, the system remained the same.

The platform of choice in the 1930s was radio – which became commonplace In households during that time, in many cases supplanting the need for a record player. The emergence of radio initially concerned record companies and artists alike. Chanan (1995: 61) explains:

> when early broadcasters used records as a matter of course, without thinking to pay anything apart from their purchase price, it was like free advertising. But after radio took off, then its growing use of recorded music threw the record companies into a schizophrenic frenzy.

If radio networks could be forced to pay royalties for playing recorded music, there was the potential for millions of dollars to flow toward the record labels; any gain, however, would be diminished by the costs of legal action. Fortuitously, the promotional value of radio became apparent and after some legal wranglings mutually beneficial arrangements were formed between the two industries.

> Decca was the first company to realise that an investment in adver-
> tisement and promotion was more than justified by the consequent
> increase in sales. The peculiarity of record-making is that once the
> break-even point is passed, the accumulation of profit is stunningly
> quick – the costs of reproduction are a small proportion of the costs
> of producing the original master disc or tape. It follows that huge
> sales of one title are much more profitable than tiny sales of scores
> of titles, and that money spent on ensuring those huge sales is thus
> a 'necessary' cost. (Frith 2006: 235)

Decca's approach was to support its output with big-budget promotion that would pay for itself by ensuring huge sales of records. This strategy became something of the norm; large-scale campaigns to promote new releases require vast sums of capital and traditionally have largely been the province of major labels.

Despite the interruptions of the Great Depression and subsequently World War II, this formulation of the music industry remained intact through to the post-war period. The star system, built on the need to drive recorded music sales promoted through radio or live performance, continues to be the basis for the industrial production of music – a process which of itself changed the construction of music. Of course, just as the development of technologies such as radio enabled that particular mode of industrialization, the emergence of the internet has provided new opportunities for music production and distribution and thus has allowed new modes of industrialization to occur. As earlier chapters have illustrated, personal computers dramatically reduced the cost of production; multitrack recording is now possible on devices that cost very little and so the costs of producing an original master have been substantially lowered. Arguably, this in itself has lessened the historical motivation for a star-driven industry model, which lowered risk and allowed the required return on initial investment to be more predictably achieved. Additionally, the costs of distribution have also significantly changed – the network has reduced that cost to essentially zero. Some would argue that marketing costs have also potentially been reduced if a musician chooses to utilize the new possibilities of music blogs and social media. Indeed, the position occupied by radio in assisting consumers with discovering new music is being encroached on by new intermediaries such as automated Facebook and Twitter updates courtesy of Spotify, recommendation services such as iTunes Genius, and that's not to mention the wealth of blogs and file-sharing services through which many discover new sounds.

The recording industry is largely concerned with meeting the demands of the market, even if that demand is massaged into being through promoting a song via radio. The industrial production processes of the twentieth-century recording industry relied on creating blockbuster hits (the rhetoric being that blockbusters offset the financial risk taken on those artists who did not sell quite as well). Before recording and broadcast technologies drastically reduced, and in some cases eliminated, the tyrannies of geographical and temporal distance, culture was largely local and niche. As Buxton (1983: 368) notes, "the development of radio technology, which also served to distribute recordings on a mass scale, corresponded with the decline of regional cultures." The eventual emergence of recording and broadcast technologies helped homogenize musical tastes, trends and audiences. As Frith (2006: 235) adds, "For the record industry … the audience was essentially anonymous."

If the recording technologies of the early and mid-twentieth century created a singular mass audience, the arrival of the internet, or perhaps more appropriately the web 2.0 paradigm, splintered that anonymous and homogenous mass. Accelerating the splintering of popular music into a range of distinctive genres, the net enabled musicians to identify and connect directly with like-minded fans. Whilst this was not a complete return to the

> anonymous, participatory and localist folk tradition [that] had largely diminished in both England and the United States by the turn of the [twentieth] century due to the breakdown of rural communities under the influence of rapid industrialisation (Buxton 1990: 367),

there has been a re-emergence of a local, participatory music culture – although the idea of "local" now revolved around shared musical interest, regardless of geography. Fans started to seek new music in new locales – online forums, file-sharing or social networking sites, and the one-size-fits-all market pushed by the recording industry was supplemented by infinite niches. Indeed, the mainstream record industry struggled to even acknowledge the diversity and depth of the newly shared experience. For example, HMV's website (an typical stalwart of the twentieth-century music economy, although now defunct) listed only a dozen broad music genres, whereas a specialist retailer such as Beatport lists twenty-three different genres within the umbrella category of electronic dance music alone.

The contemporary audience has more in common with that of the pre-industrial era, spreading out into niches, although these are characterized by interest rather than geography. The mass market is gradually dissolving into a multitude of smaller, focused markets. Chris Anderson (2006) argues that although the record labels had "cracked the commercial code", the block-buster approach was an anomaly and its era has now passed:

> the audience is turning to a distribution medium that doesn't favor the hits alone. We are abandoning the tyranny of the top and becoming a niche nation again, defined not by our geography but by our interests … The mass market is yielding to a million minimarkets. Hits will always be with us, but they have lost their monopoly. Blockbusters must now compete with an infinite number of niche offerings, which can be distributed just as easily.

Writing for *Forbes*, entertainment lawyer Richard Busch (2012) supports Anderson's assertion; during the 1980s blockbuster albums were in abundance in the USA, with 84 individual releases achieving sales of five million copies and 19 exceeding ten million copies. In 2009, however, the best-selling album was Taylor Swift's *Fearless* (2008), which sold (only) 2.36 million copies, whilst 2011 saw Adele's *21* (2011) hailed as a blockbuster with sales of 5.82 million copies.

Although its scale may be smaller than in previous decades, the blockbuster hit still exists and the authors do not expect that to change any time soon; we simply suggest that the blockbuster hit is no longer the only (or even ultimate) measure of success and that the affordances of the network present numerous alternative understandings of what it means to be a successful artist in the twenty-first century. For example, (as of April 2012) Gotye's single 'Somebody That I Used To Know' (2011) reportedly sold 4.5 million copies (Smirke 2012), but Canadian independents Walk Off the Earth's cover version (2012) received 102,985,360 views on YouTube between January and May 2012. Clearly there is no direct equivalence between a sale and a YouTube view, but they both provide measures of popularity, indicators of "stardom". The determination of success can be highly individualistic and although this is largely dealt with in the following chapter, it is worth noting here that success is multifaceted and troublesome to map in the networked environment. What *is* the worth of a million YouTube views or Facebook "Likes"?

A Star Is Born 2.0

The new technologies make it possible to create, distribute and market music much more cheaply than has ever been the case. And in the new environment, the necessity for an industry model built on the star system is open to question. But mere possibility does not change existing cultural practice or alter long-held cultural habits. Not only does the existing music industry have inertia that cannot easily be shifted (business practices, infrastructure, profit motives and attitudes that are built entirely around a star system) but the public is comfortable with the idea of pop stars. It provides an easy basis for music discovery, a form of imagined community and, importantly, serves as an aspirational model for musicians. So whilst it is possible for musicians and their audiences to move away from the twentieth-century blockbuster/star model, there is too much invested, in terms of both culture and capital, for that shift to happen immediately.

The more likely short-term impact of the new technologies and practices is a bifurcated industry. The affordances of digital computers and networks will be embraced by some to invert the existing music business, particularly as they empower those who would otherwise not have been able to succeed as musicians. This will be further discussed in detail in the next chapter. Simultaneously, those same technologies will be adopted by the existing industrial behemoths and used to expedite the existing industrial processes. This chapter is concerned with musicians and record labels who have understood that the new technologies are enabling ones for those who already work in the star system. Rather than kill that particular industrial model, they provide new ways to extend and embrace the old.

The Music 2.0 meme is largely centred on the ability for musicians to achieve success via the internet. Its veracity is normally demonstrated by citing the example of a band that has found fame and fortune without the backing of a large music label. Often described as a "MySpace phenomenon", the Arctic Monkeys are held up as an exemplar of how that social network provided the mechanism for the band's success (their debut album was the fastest-selling album in UK pop history). Indeed, Laura Barton (2005) asked, "Have the Arctic Monkeys changed the music business?"

Whilst this is a valid question, the answer is complex. The music business as we know it was still required to propel the Arctic Monkeys to its level of success. Arguably, MySpace merely served as a crowd-sourced A&R scouting environment – a place where record companies could find evidence that a band had the potential to sell (Laughey 2007: 180). For the Arctic Monkeys, MySpace provided a forum for their early fans to connect and share files from CDs given away at gigs, demonstrating that the band did indeed have a fan base. After all, although the Arctic Monkeys are signed to an independent label, they are published through a major label (EMI) in many territories including the USA. So whilst the internet enabled their discovery by the music industry, in many ways they are very much a product of that star-driven system.

Another example that illustrates the complexity of the current environment is Justin Bieber. For those readers over twenty-five, Bieber is a Canadian pop phenomenon, whose trajectory towards fame began with a series of YouTube videos. As a child, he was successful in local singing competitions, and his mother posted videos of his performances onto YouTube – where he developed something of a fan base. Broader fame came when he was discovered by Scooter Braun, a record-industry executive (with So So Def), who stumbled across a Bieber song while searching for videos of another singer. Braun tracked down the artist and became his manager – introducing him to established artists such as Usher and signing him to Island Records. From that point, Bieber's career took off, with a string of hit singles and a smash album, a world tour, television appearances (notably on CSI playing a troubled teen who was eventually killed), a 3D biopic feature film and a fragrance; "Girl-friend" reportedly sold one bottle per minute in the first week it went on sale (MTV 2012). By the middle of 2011, Forbes ranked him the second-highest-paid celebrity under thirty years old, having earned $53 million in a 12-month period.

At face value, the Justin Bieber story is the twenty-first-century expression of a traditional pop career. Just as the star system has created superstars over the last fifty years, the industry manufactured the Justin Bieber sensation; it created the product, conjured up the airplay (radio and television), negotiated the exposure (including performing for the US president) and leveraged the total marketing impact, taking advantage of its cultural power to commod-itize the latest teeny-bopper sensation. And as with any other such sensation, the process created as many haters as fans; Bieber's videos became both the most viewed and the most disliked videos on YouTube.

But the Bieber story has a twenty-first-century twist. He was not discov-ered playing covers in a seedy bar, but on YouTube; YouTube continues to be an important outlet and his videos there have been viewed more than 240 million times. Braun had a strategy:

> I wanted to build him up more on YouTube first. [he said] We sup-plied more content. I said: "Justin, sing like there's no one in the room. But let's not use expensive cameras. We'll give it to kids, let them do the work, so that they feel like it's theirs." (Hoffman 2009: 2)

Bieber's popularity was built not on radio and music television, but on the back of an enormous social network campaign. At one stage, Bieber-related tweets made up 3 per cent of the content on Twitter, and, with in excess of 21 million followers at the time of writing, he was considered the most influen-tial individual in the social networking realm, more so than the US President (Rushe 2011). As Aston Kutcher – the first Tweeter to gain more than a mil-lion followers (*The Guardian*, 21 April 2009) – points out, a key strength of

Twitter lies in the direct connections established between celebrities and fans (Coyle 2009). Tweets emanating from his official feed are a primary method of communication between Bieber and his fans: "It's a giant chat room where you can connect with your friends and followers, letting them know 'What's happening?', as Twitter asks, all day and all night long" (Cross 2011: 54). That direct connection has consequences. In 2009, Scooter Braun was criticized by police (and eventually arrested) for not tweeting fast enough to inform fans that an appearance by Bieber at the Roosevelt Field shopping mall in Long Island, New York, was cancelled (Bolger 2000). A near-riot ensued, leading to numerous injuries and at least one arrest. Twitter was key in both fuelling and dissuading attendance by fans – Bieber's Twitter feed maintained that he would be attending while Braun was compelled by security and police personnel to tweet that the event was cancelled.

Justin Bieber exemplifies the new star system at work. Just as there is still a clear market for music that reaches a mass audience, there is still a place for the star system that has served the music industry so well for the last century. But Bieber demonstrates how that star system has evolved. Not only does it utilize the twentieth-century mechanisms of radio, television, cinema and the press, but it fully exploits the twenty-first-century opportunities of the internet and builds on the affordances of social media; it has, in some ways, colonized social media networks, giving them industry credibility. For example, as well as a presence on the key social networks, the music industry explored interesting hybrids. Paramount Pictures, the studio behind the *Justin Bieber: Never Say Never* (2011) movie, presented its live premiere on Livestream, which also streamed it for free via Facebook and had a minute-by-minute coverage on Twitter (McHugh 2011). The premiere was available globally and was the first movie premiere that Paramount had launched in that manner.

And, of course, there is the IPhone app — or more accurately apps. Whilst there is no doubt an official Justin Bieber app, a quick search of Apple's app store uncovers well over 100 apps related to the teenage pop sensation, ranging from a photobooth-style app which places his distinctive hairstyle over your chosen image to an app which allows users to hit his head or slap him to elicit sound effects. This fan-created expression mirrors that of the web – where countless sites, blogs and Facebook pages are devoted to his worship. More intriguingly, the backlash against his fame (which is common for many teen pop stars) also found its expression online. In an example of online space demonstrating the reality of audience diversity, Bieber became the target of bloggers, YouTubers and Facebookers. His YouTube videos have been hacked and redirected to adult websites, rumours of his death were circulated and there was a (successful) campaign to push "Justin Bieber Syphilis" to the top of the Google Trends search list. Users of the notorious image board 4chan were particularly engaged and drove a campaign to send Bieber to North Korea as part of his world tour – a relatively simple prank which was a coordinated attempt to influence a web-based competition to nominate a bonus country for the artist's tour.

Arguably, in this particular case, such a digital presence has accelerated the pace of Bieber's fame. Whilst the music industry has created instant stars in the past such as the Monkees or NSync (Knopper 2009: 80–104), the new technologies mean that it is no longer able to exercise the same control over the star in question – nor to control the reaction to its creation:

> Usher comments that while he and Bieber were both signed at the same age, he "had the chance to ramp up [his] success, where this has happened to Bieber abruptly." As a result, Usher, Braun, Bieber's bodyguard Kenny, and other adults surrounding Bieber constantly coach him on handling fame and his public image. (Hoffman 2009)

The Arctic Monkeys and Justin Bieber are examples of musicians who were discovered via the internet, and then picked up and marketed within the music industry's star system – often using the new media technologies as vehicles for publicity and distribution. They exemplify the ways in which the star system continues to be a significant part of the music industry, and in which the music industry capitalizes on the affordances of the new technologies. Clearly, the internet is not solely the domain of the struggling independent musician, but is sometimes merely another tool in the arsenal of the mainstream media marketing machine.

Another key example of this is Susan Boyle, who appeared on the televised variety contest *Britain's Got Talent* in April 2009. In what (with hindsight) appears to be a carefully constructed set piece designed to lower expectations and maximize the dramatic effect, she was made out to be a slightly eccentric example of the show's no-hopers – another random amateur desperate to be on television. But when she sang "I Dreamed A Dream", the audience and the judges went crazy. Apparently, she could sing after all and suddenly Susan Boyle was everywhere – in the newspapers and magazines, on US talk shows and on television all over the world. The internet was a key part of that dissemination. Videos of her appearance were viewed tens of millions of times on YouTube and according to Visible Measures topped the viral video charts (until she was replaced by Invisible Children's *Kony 2012* campaign), taking just nine days to surpass 100 million views (Visible Measures 2012). Boyle's Facebook page drew over 1.6 million "Likes" and she became a Twitter star when Ashton Kutcher promoted the video clip. Susan Boyle's first album was one of the biggest sellers in the world for 2009, and, thanks to pre-orders, *I Dreamed A Dream* (2009) was Amazon's number one CD three months before it was even released. Readers of *Time* magazine voted her the seventh most influential person in the world in April 2010. Susan Boyle's stardom demonstrates the complexity of the new music environment. It was an event that played out through the internet – on YouTube, Facebook, Twitter and Wikipedia – but also through old-fashioned industries such as television and radio, newspapers, magazines and the sale of CDs. She was clearly created by a star system that has its roots in the early twentieth century, but which now uses tools that were unimaginable back then. Her story is a clear example of how the internet is as useful within the star system as it is to those who resist that approach to creating and popularizing music.

If You Can Make It Here, You Can Make It Anywhere

One of the most interesting points to be derived from the examples of Bieber and Boyle is that the same online tools are accessible to any artist regardless of any relationship with a recording label. You don't need to work in marketing to promote via Twitter. You don't need to be a writer or a journalist to blog. You don't need to be a record label to distribute music online. The apparently equal access to these tools has many implications for the traditional relationships between artists and labels, particularly those who may have already been chewed up (and sometimes spat out) by the star system.

The internet presents a key opportunity for many artists to regain control. Just as the major labels have used the new technologies for marketing and distribution, they have been adopted by established stars, many of whom see the internet as a means to bypass the control that the industry has had on their careers. Bands with sufficient profile are distributing their music without having to resort to bricks-and-mortar distribution deals. Radiohead's Thom Yorke told *Time* magazine, "I like the people at our record company, but the time is at hand when you have to ask why anyone needs one" (Tyrangiel 2007). Thus, in 2007 Radiohead distributed *In Rainbows* (2007) through its own website. Having concluded their contract with EMI, the band made the album freely available online in an "honesty-box" format (asking fans to pay what they thought the music was worth), with a reported 1.2 million downloads in the first three weeks. The exact income generated by the self-release of *In Rainbows* is unknown. Some reports suggest that the majority of users opted to pay nothing at all (David 2010: 135, 175), while others claim "most people [decided] on a normal retail price with very few trying to buy it for a penny" (*BBC News* 2007a). In an interview with David Byrne for *Wired*, Thom Yorke said,

> In terms of digital income, we've made more money out of this
> record than out of all the other Radiohead albums put together, for-
> ever – in terms of anything on the Net. And that's nuts. It's partly
> due to the fact that EMI wasn't giving us any money for digital sales.
> All the contracts signed in a certain era have none of that stuff.
> (Byrne and Yorke 2007)

Regardless of the financial success of the digital self-release, Radiohead then
went on to license the album to various labels around the world. The CD
release went to number one in both the UK and the USA, among other territories. Arguably, the download project was a sophisticated promotion for the
CD (Wikström 2009: 110; Harvey 2011).

Nine Inch Nails is another example. Having established itself as a bona fide
recording star through several label-backed releases, in 2008 NIN pushed new
boundaries. *Ghosts I–IV* (2008) was made available through the band's official
website in a number of formats, ranging from free downloads to a limited-
edition "Ultra Deluxe" package which cost $300 (and which sold out its 2,500
copies in three days). This marked the beginning of a range of innovative
releases that have included the distribution of digital files that allow fans to
remix songs, iPhone apps and extensive use of Creative Commons licences.
Creative Commons is an initiative spearheaded by Lawrence Lessig and the
Center for the Public Domain. Through a range of opt-in licences that permit
re-use and distribution of copyrighted works, Creative Commons promotes
a richer public domain by offering an alternative to the default "all rights
reserved" statement.

And some musicians are keen to go it alone. For many years, some artists have regarded record labels as an unloved necessity. Janis Ian, a recording artist for nearly fifty years, comments: "I've created 20+ albums for major
labels, and I've never once received a royalty check that didn't show I owed
them money" (Ian 2002). Courtney Love recounts how Toni Braxton was
forced to file for bankruptcy despite selling $188 million worth of CDs, and
TLC, similarly bankrupt, ended up with liabilities of $3.5 million (Nelson 2001:
164). Mick Hucknall – at first glance an unlikely pioneer in this area – started
simplyred.com in 1994 following his split from Warner because he "got sick of
them taking all the money" (BBC May 2006). In what initially seems a strange
manoeuvre, UK rock band Def Leppard are re-recording some of their hits.
The band have been unsuccessfully battling with Universal over royalties for
digital downloads (Graff 2012); not willing to back down, they have decided
to re-record hits such as 'Pour Some Sugar On Me' (1987) (which in 1988
peaked at number 2 in the *Billboard* charts). According to Nielsen SoundScan,
Def Leppard had sold 21,000 copies of the song in the USA by July 2012 and

planned to release more "forgeries" in an effort to profit from their back catalogue in the digital market.

Established stars have explored the potential of the new music networks
and have established presences across the gamut of online outlets from
iTunes to Topspin to Spotify. However, despite the best efforts of musicians
and labels, it is undeniable that there has been a shift in attitudes. In a forum
post on the NIN website, Trent Reznor advised artists to actively give away
their music for free to promote sales of deluxe and limited-edition products.
He proposes,

> Forget thinking you are going to make any real money from record
> sales. Make your record cheaply (but great) and GIVE IT AWAY. As
> an artist you want as many people as possible to hear your work ...
> The point is this: music IS free whether you want to believe that
> or not. Every piece of music you can think of is available free right
> now a click away. This is a fact – it sucks as the musician BUT
> THAT'S THE WAY IT IS (for now). So ... have the public get what
> they want FROM YOU instead of a torrent site and garner good
> will in the process (plus build your database [of fan contacts]).
> (Reznor 2007)

Whilst digital sales figures have recently surpassed physical sales, the reality
is that a large amount of digital music is distributed without any real commercial gain to the artist or label. But rather than bemoan the comparison to
the heady peaks of the 1980s and 1990s, let us view earlier music histories as
a useful precedent. Arguably, the sale of recorded music has been the dominant revenue generator of the industry only for the peculiar period of the late
twentieth century – prior music markets consisted of a combination of performance, publishing and recording sales, which is arguably just as natural a
mix.

Indeed, given that the late-twentieth-century music industry was built on
the control of scarce physical goods and it has now been forced to confront a
future in which scarcity is no longer possible, let alone manageable, then musicians are confronted with the need to explore how best to provide a product
that people value enough to pay money for. Clear examples of this abound.
Sales of recorded music may appear to be suffering, but live performances
have become their bread and butter for many musicians (especially unsigned,
DIY bands). Whereas touring was once a means to promote an album, today
the opposite is true. The perceived economic value of recorded music is depre-
ciating while the value of live performances has risen. David Bowie proposed
that the increasing ubiquity of recorded music would result in touring being
the only remaining unique experience.

> Music itself is going to become like running water or electricity ...
> You'd better be prepared for doing a lot of touring because that's
> really the only unique situation that's going to be left. It's terribly
> exciting. But on the other hand it doesn't matter if you think it's
> exciting or not; it's what's going to happen. (Pareles 2002: 2)

While fans are apparently less willing to pay for MP3 files, they continue
to pay significant amounts of money to see their favourite bands live. For
example, in 1990 it cost £25 to see the Rolling Stones at Wembley – a figure
considered steep at the time. In 2006, however, it cost fans £150 for a standard seat or £350 for a premium view of the stage (Sandall 2007: 31). Such
high prices did not appear to deter fans, with big tours regularly selling out.
As Bowie says, the resurgence in the popularity of live performances is arguably a response to the ubiquity of recorded music in the digital age – the
scarcity of the live act frames its fan value. This reinforces a view shared by
many bands who now consider recorded music to be of less financial value
than the live performance; MP3s and CDs are increasingly viewed as promotional tools dispatched to draw fans to live performances. There, they transform into customers paying for the initial ticket and then for merchandise
that includes the traditional T-shirt, but also singles, albums, and in some
cases a recording of the gig they just saw – the ultimate fan memento.

For example, Peter Frawley, production manager for New Found Fre-
quency (NFF), stated that thirty minutes after a concert for the Dalai Lama
held at a 13,000-capacity venue, he had produced and sold 8,000 copies
of the performance. In June 2007 half the audience at a sell-out Choco-
late Starfish reunion performance bought CDs of the gig they had just seen
(Murfett 2007). Media technology company Aderra offers its clients on-site
recording as well as USB wristbands to which new content can be wirelessly
downloaded. These business models are supported by music futurists Kusek
and Leonhard, who argue that

> many aspects of digital music (and "digital music marketing") and
> live entertainment will be converging down the road, and that the
> two sectors will be much more intertwined than music/CD retail
> and touring could ever have been ... [b]ecause *digital music is
> mobile*, and as intangible and experience-based as the concert expe-
> rience. (Kuseck and Leonhard 2005: 115)

As another example, British post-hardcore band Enter Shikari played 700
gigs between 2003 and 2007 and used its own website and MySpace as central points for disseminating music and information about live performances.
These factors, coupled with word of mouth spread by fans, led Enter Shikari

in November 2006 to become the second unsigned band ever to sell out the London Astoria (Sandall 2007: 28). Interestingly, the band's DIY roots and "no need" attitude towards the major labels succumbed when faced with the prospect of touring America: "America's just too big for us to do things on our own." Enter Shikari signed with a major label for US release, but are adhering to their roots in Europe. "As long as it ain't broke in the UK, I'm not inclined to fix it," said the band's manager, Ian Johnson (Lear n.d.).

Live performances, publishing, licensing and merchandise are growing areas, something the record labels acknowledge with moves to capitalize on these alternative revenue streams. An example is the multiple rights (also known as the "360-degree") contract, in which the labels manage not only music recording and publishing rights, but also skim percentages off touring and merchandising revenues. Other examples include arrangements that have extended artists' reach into new commercial opportunities such as fragrances and underwear. Such ventures are not unprecedented – the notion of artist as brand has been propagated for years, by many artists including David Bowie, who issued "Bowie Bonds" in 1997, set up his own ISP in 1998 and launched Bowiebanc in 2000.

The danger for labels, though, is that other companies might intrude on their turf. The most high-profile example of this change in priorities is Madonna's business realignment. In October 2006, Madonna announced that she would no longer be continuing her 25-year association with Warner Music and had negotiated an all-in-one 360-degree contract encompassing "new albums, tours, merchandise, sponsorship, TV shows and films" with Live Nation, a company whose main business is touring. As she stated,

> The paradigm in the music business has shifted and as an artist and a businesswoman, I have to move with that shift … For the first time in my career, the way that my music can reach my fans is unlimited. I've never wanted to think in a limited way and with this new partnership, the possibilities are endless. (*BBC News* 2007b)

Within a fortnight of Madonna announcing her new affiliation with Live Nation, the company began negotiations for the acquisition of Signatures Network, an enterprise that deals in marketing and licensing merchandise rights for over 125 artists including Justin Timberlake, Kanye West, Black Eyed Peas and U2 (Lauria 2008). In addition to concert promotion, Live Nation deals with the full gamut of entertainment promotion including ticketing and merchandise. When the perceived value of recorded music is at historical lows, will the culturally significant position once occupied by the major labels be filled by companies such as Live Nation that have touring and promotions at the heart of their business? Live Nation signed several 360-degree deals between 2007 and 2010, but since then has not ventured further into the market. The model it operated, however, has proven popular with the major labels (White 2012). According to the BPI, 360 deals contributed £76 million of extra revenue to the UK recording industry in 2011, accounting for a fifth of its total revenue (Ingham 2012).

Of course, individual artists have different responses to change. What works for Madonna will not be appropriate for an unsigned new artist. It is worth noting that in 2011 Madonna signed a new three-album deal with Interscope Records, a subsidiary of Universal Music Group. She is, however, concurrently maintaining business relations with Live Nation. It is clear that whilst the new technologies make more direct relationships with fans possible, somebody still has to build those relationships, and this still requires resources that smaller artists often do not have.

Everyone's a Critic

But the new media technologies have also expanded other parts of the music business. As seen in the examples above, social media have become a key part of the marketing strategies of the major labels. Whilst YouTube, MySpace, Facebook and Twitter can – and are – being used by non-mainstream artists (see Chapter 6 for more analysis), the social media space is also an integral part of mainstream popular music. Indeed, there is obvious tension concerning how the expanding social media outlets are used. We have already pointed to Facebook's foray into music but nowhere is this movement clearer than in the realm of music blogs. To some, blogs build on the tradition of fanzines, allowing an authentic expression of a music scene, generated from the ground up by active participants in the scene. To others, they are a reconfiguration of music criticism, providing a space to supplement (or sometimes replace) the rich history of published critics in magazines such as *Rolling Stone* – publications that have always had a role in both critiquing and promoting particular music, in a tense symbiotic relationship with record labels. In some readings, the social media approaches began as alternatives to those established publications, allowing new critical voices to emerge, unencumbered by the need to do the industry's bidding. But as the public relations arms of the record industry intrude upon the space, bloggers find themselves torn between the temptation of establishing relationships with the industry and retaining the authenticity of the initial motivation for the blog.

There is some suggestion that in particular music scenes, music blogs have become what Bruns (2005: 2) calls the "gatewatchers" – providing an entrée for musicians looking to gain fame and fortune. Indeed, the last few years have seen the emergence of "blog bands" – those discovered and made famous thanks to the hype generated by music blogs, whose popularity is generated through the network dynamics of the internet. Clap Your Hands Say Yeah, a Canadian indie band, came to prominence on the indie scene after they circulated a number of MP3s in the blogosphere (Bemis 2005). The inclusion of National and Sufjan Stevens on the 'Top 40 Bands in America' blog in 2005 was also attributed to the buzz that came after exposure on a network of music blogs. A key example of the influence carried by music blogs is *Pitchfork*. Created by Ray Schreiber in 1995, *Pitchfork* is credited with the ability to make or break artists (du Lac 2006: 1). For example, in 2004, after *Pitchfork* nominated Arcade Fire's *Funeral* (2004) as the best album of 2004, the band attained mainstream success and toured with U2 and David Bowie. Arguably, off the back of *Pitchfork*'s endorsement, *Funeral* became the fastest-selling record ever released by Arcade Fire's label, Merge Records. Other artists to benefit from *Pitchfork*'s influence include Modest Mouse and Broken Social Scene. *Pitchfork*'s boosting does, however, have a flip side that can negatively impact reviewed artists. *Travistan* (2004), the solo album by Dismemberment Plan's frontman Travis Morrison, was awarded a flat zero out of ten and the results were tangible:

> College radio programmers cooled to his new project, a record store in Texas initially refused to stock the CD, and fans suddenly decided they probably shouldn't like Morrison anymore, either. (du Lac 2006: 3)

Of course, *Pitchfork* is just one of a multitude of music review sites and blogs, but the rise of alternative locales for music criticism has coincided with a decline in the traditional music press. Circulation figures indicate that *NME* and *Q* lost nearly 20 per cent of their respective readerships during 2011 (Sweney 2012). Although *NME* was lucky enough to be compensated with an exponential rise in visitors to its website, *Word* magazine lost 22.5 per cent of its readership during 2009 and finally closed down in the middle of 2012 after nine years of publication. Sean Elder (2002), in "The Death of Rolling Stone", suggests that such declines are due to difficulties in finding an audience in a fragmenting market – a market more easily addressed by niche blogs than general-readership music magazines. Moreover, the broader debates about citizen journalism have spilled over into Gillmor's reconsideration of the role of the music critic as "the former audience joins the party" (2006: 136).

Complicating the new role of music criticism, the ubiquity of music online makes it increasingly simple for audiences to experience music for themselves rather than make a purchasing decision based on a description written by a critic. Jonah Weiner (2009) argues,

> The value of the music reviewer has always been split between con-
> sumer service (should people plunk down cash for this CD?) and
> art criticism (what's the CD about?), but of late the balance has
> shifted from the former toward the latter—answering the question
> of whether to buy an album isn't much use when, for a lot of listen-
> ers, the music is effectively free.

In the equation of music discovery emphasis has shifted from cost to time. While much music can be heard for free online, filtering the heavenly jukebox to our tastes is key, and the convenience of recommendation in the same (vir-tual) space as music acquisition ostensibly has contributed to the decline of the print music press. Further, the recommendation engines that are integrated into services such as iTunes, Last.FM, Pandora and Spotify provide an alterna-tive method for audiences to discover music.

Although filters such as music blogs and algorithm-fuelled recommenda-tion systems are no panacea and cannot entirely replace the traditional music press, they are indicative of the broader changes that are impacting all aspects of the music industry. Whilst many of those changes are enabling the major labels to engage with audiences in new ways, they are also allowing musi-cians to bypass those labels entirely. For such musicians, Music 2.0 holds tre-mendous appeal; given their existing fan base, it suggests that the traditional distribution infrastructure is not necessary. Likewise, younger musicians see Music 2.0 as a way to bypass the apparently arbitrary decision-making pro-cesses of the majors. It is natural for a generation that has not known a world without the internet to embrace those technologies unreservedly. The next chapter will explore the alternatives.

6   What about Me?

> Whenever I talk to a band who are about to sign with a major label, I always end up thinking of them in a particular context. I imagine a trench, about four feet wide and five feet deep, maybe sixty yards long, filled with runny, decaying shit. I imagine these people, some of them good friends, some of them barely acquaintances, at one end of this trench. I also imagine a faceless industry lackey at the other end holding a fountain pen and a contract waiting to be signed. Nobody can see what's printed on the contract. It's too far away, and besides, the shit stench is making everybody's eyes water. The lackey shouts to everybody that the first one to swim the trench gets to sign the contract. Everybody dives in the trench and they struggle furiously to get to the other end. Two people arrive simultaneously and begin wrestling furiously, clawing each other and dunking each other under the shit. Eventually, one of them capitulates, and there's only one contestant left. He reaches for the pen, but the Lackey says "Actually, I think you need a little more development. Swim again, please. Backstroke." And he does of course. (Albini 1994).

In the context of popular music, how is success defined? For many artists, the major-label deal is symbolic of success; "making it" in the music industry means a recording contract. This broad-brush approach suggests that achieving the dream of the major-label deal, radio play and tours constitutes success. Certainly, multinational television franchises of *X Factor*, *Idol* and *<insert your country>'s Got Talent* exploit this popular dream and demonstrate that it's not just aspirants who subscribe to the dream, but the audience too wants them to succeed on those particular terms.

But, in reality, success comes in all shapes and sizes, and may not be a fixed notion for any individual artist or band. Arguably, whether or not success has been achieved is subjective and despite perceptions from elsewhere, only the artists themselves can judge their success or otherwise. For example, some musicians may measure success as regular Saturday night gigs on the local pub circuit or selling two thousand copies of a laptop-produced techno track on Beatport. Others discount any achievement other than multi-million unit sales of a recorded artefact. Of course, the subjectivity of such descriptions of success matters little (except to those directly involved) – but for the fact that a particular notion of success has been captured within discourses around the music industry to support a specific narrative designed to preserve historical business models. In that narrative, the internet has enabled the rise of music piracy, preventing musicians from achieving success, as measured in terms of recorded music sales. Setting aside the fact that much record-label "success" has not flowed onto the musicians themselves, this chapter rejects that singular notion of success and argues that the internet actually enables new possibilities for musicians that many would embrace as successful achievements.

The reality is that, for musicians, success has always been subjective. Even before there were music superstars, there have been those making a living from music outside of the limelight. Indeed, before there were recording technologies, musicians derived their incomes from live performance. Liszt and Paganini were the "stars" of nineteenth-century music and achieved fame and fortune, but the German composer Flotow told how most musicians worked in the 1800s. Describing the Parisian live music scene, he wrote:

> ... one makes several appearances in the course of winter, and then, at the beginning of Lent, one announces a concert and sends a dozen high-priced tickets ... to the hostess of every salon at which one has played. That is the usual practice ... The cost of such a concert is negligible. It is given on a profit-sharing basis, takes place in daylight, which saves the expense of lighting, and no heating is necessary, because the audience turn up in their outdoor clothes. Placards at street-corners are unnecessary, and in any case would serve no purpose. Nor is there any need for a box office, and there is hardly even any need to have an attendant on duty at the door to collect the tickets ... The audiences consist of habitues of the various salons and always give the virtuosos, whom they have already met, and the music they play, most of which they already know, the warmest possible reception. Any artist who is ambitious can easily maintain himself in Paris in this agreeable fashion, without wasting much time or trouble over it. (Kracauer 1972: 47)

Whilst live performance has continued as a major income source for many musicians, the twentieth-century recording industry has quantified success by measuring the number of retail units of recorded artefacts shipped and the revenue generated from those sales. The use of sales charts as both a measure of success and a marketing tool for new music is a feature of recent popular music – and one dominated by major record labels that have the resources to promote and distribute their wares. The new media technologies have afforded further opportunities for artists on major labels (explored in the previous chapter) but also provide alternative possibilities for independent artists to achieve an "agreeable" living. Of course, independent success was possible before Music 2.0, but – just as in other media industries – the new technologies have provided greater access to tools of production and distribution; the new digital tools have exposed a previously invisible mass of musicians worldwide, allowing them new ways to succeed as musicians.

This chapter is concerned with the independent artist and the possibilities that exist to connect directly with audiences and monetize creativity. Based on one-on-one interviews with a range of musicians, contextualized with a broader online survey, we explore some of the innovations of Music 2.0 fostered at a grass-roots level. The feedback from musicians is clear – by leveraging the new technologies artists are able to craft careers that look very different from traditional pathways. Our research amplifies other examples of musicians, case studies that suggest new approaches to musical success. Of course, not every musician with a Facebook page will become a global superstar, but it is possible to earn – to paraphrase Flotow – an "agreeable" living. And it appears that many are doing so. For example, Jeff Price, founder and CEO of TuneCore, says "Every single month I'm looking at thousands upon thousands of artists, some generating just $100, but many generating $20,000, $30,000. And that's not an anomaly anymore" (Sydell 2011). It certainly does not appear to be an anomaly. Pandora founder Tim Westergren (2012) blogged that Donnie McClurkin, French Montana and Grupo Bryndis (three artists unheard of by the authors) stood to receive performance fees from the internet radio site of $100,228, $138,567 and $114,192, respectively. Westergren added:

> And that's just the tip of the iceberg. For over two thousand artists Pandora will pay over $10,000 dollars each over the next 12 months (including one of my favorites, the late jazz pianist Oscar Peterson), and for more than 800 we'll pay over $50,000, more than the income of the average American household. For top earners like Coldplay, Adele, Wiz Khalifa, Jason Aldean and others Pandora is already paying over $1 million each. Drake and Lil Wayne are fast approaching a $3 million annual rate each.

> This revenue stream is meaningful. I remember the many years I spent in a band when earning an additional thousand dollars a month would have been the difference between making music an avocation and a hobby. We're talking here about the very real possibility of creating, for the first time ever, an actual musicians middle class.

Despite evidence seemingly to the contrary, there are those who reject the equalizing effects of the new technologies and argue that their net effect is a negative one, but we argue otherwise. For the authors, Music 2.0 represents displacement not replacement (Benedikt 1991) and that displacement encompasses both continuity and transformation (Meikle and Young 2012: 7–11). Clearly, the new technologies are not a panacea, but rather they provide new opportunities and affordances with their own limitations and challenges. However, overall, we are convinced that musicians now have a greater opportunity for being musicians; how that opportunity is grasped remains, as ever, in the lap of the gods.

Making the Invisible Visible

The social implications of new technologies are seldom understood properly without the benefit of hindsight. In 2007, the authors surveyed over 200 artists, ranging from those recording tracks in their bedroom studios, through those with gigging pub bands, to those who had achieved Top Ten chart success. The questions posed by our online survey were derived from a number of qualitative interviews conducted with a diverse representation of artists predominantly from – but not limited to – Australia. With the benefit of hindsight some of the responses and attitudes seem anything from obvious to passé (especially when it comes to MySpace), but the data we obtained were invaluable in helping us draw out a picture of how musicians are slowly becoming visible through the networked ecology.

The technological innovations of the last twenty years have created an environment that invites disruption. As we have previously described, the internet, web and networked personal computer have converged into the ubiquitous post-PC media device, and the twentieth-century paradigms of production, consumption and distribution are under considerable threat. The mp3 format, Napster and eventual emergence of iTunes, Spotify and the like provoked the major labels into adapting their business models to embrace the digital realm, albeit grudgingly at first. The industry typified by Doug Morris as one that "just didn't know what to do" (Mnookin 2007) has largely been replaced by a slightly hipper traditional recording industry able to negotiate the digital economy, securing deals and partnerships with the new intermediaries. The industry is now even happy to cast aside the high-street megastores that used to provide its bread-and-butter sales, as exemplified by the closure of the iconic Tower Records in the USA and the downsizing of the previously ubiquitous HMV chain of stores in the UK. In January 2013 HMV's death knell rang as the company went into administration. Even anti-piracy efforts appear less intensive than in previous years; between 2009 and 2011 the RIAA's budget has been cut in half, with its legal fees dropping from $16.5 million to $2.34 million. (The tax filing indicating this can be found at http://www.scribd.com/doc/103124458/RIAA-2010-2011-form-990.) Contested, but still evolving, it is clear that life remains in the major labels; they still retain the means to make and break stars, market them effectively and create mainstream pop monsters with enormous money-making ability. The new technologies have not destroyed that part of the industry (and indeed have enabled it to explore new revenue models), but they have expanded another. Artists unable to gain the attention of the A&R folk in the major labels have at their disposal marketing and distribution mechanisms that are relatively accessible and genuinely global.

Of its many affordances, the internet's ability to make the invisible visible (Meikle and Young 2012: 127–47) is one of its most apparent. The shift from a heavily controlled media-scape, watched over by gatekeeper arbiters of standards, to an apparent free-for-all where the blurred lines between producers and consumers have resulted in a plethora of previously inaccessible content becoming much more readily available. Although some such as Keen (2007: 27) might argue that Music 2.0 results in a "decline in quality", we simply suggest that the network shines a light where there has been no light before. Irrespective of the specific genre or performance, it will be there. People who make music will post it, and with a potential global audience the possibility of finding sufficient fans is greater than it has been in the history of performed music. In the comparatively recent past, unsigned acts might struggle to be seen – only the regulars at the local bar would have the opportunity to appreciate their talent, and for many otherwise deserving acts, obscurity was a near-certain fate. Today, however, examples abound of musicians who have bypassed the star system and carved a niche for themselves; a middle class of musicians have established a reasonable career and "agreeable" living from music without necessarily being global stars.

Local bands can leverage the new technologies in ways that were unimaginable a decade ago. One (hyper)local example exemplifies the possibilities. Head in a Jar is a Sydney-based thrash metal band – a genre that had its heyday back in the 1980s. As with many bands in the last thirty years, they self-released a four-track EP – and the band gives away CD copies of *Atomic Circus* (2011) at local gigs. Again, this is a practice that has historical precedents (once the duplication of CDs became affordable in the late twentieth century). What is different now in March 2013 is that Head in a Jar has 444 "Likes" on Facebook, a video on YouTube and distributes digitally on iTunes alongside thrash metal's big four – Anthrax, Metallica, Megadeth and Slayer. Whilst not an enormous online presence in absolute terms, and clearly not a direct rival to those big four thrash metal bands, Head in a Jar is now visible – fans of the genre can track down their releases with a few keystrokes, and the band has the potential for global exposure via word of mouth. After all, there is a significant difference between the number of potential thrash metal fans in Sydney and the number in the world.

My Niche or Yours?

As we have previously discussed, the star system requires scale. Record labels create superstars by appealing to mass audiences, hoping to engage them sufficiently to extract a few dollars from many of them. The resources required to market blockbuster hits mean that few artists are elevated to superstar status. Moreover, the cost of such an enterprise often means that many seldom see much return; popularity does not always translate into wealth. According to Peter Spellman, Director for Career Development at Berklee College of Music, nine out of ten "new releases for major labels never recoup their production costs" (Sibley 2001: 2). In 2001 Courtney Love argued that of "the 32,000 new releases each year, only 250 sell more than 10,000 copies. And less than 30 go platinum" (Love 2001). Indeed, some successful artists including Courtney Love and Janis Ian suggest that the star system did very little for them. Ian writes that she makes the bulk of her income from live touring, "playing for 80–1500 people a night, 200–300 nights a year" (Ian 2002). Our interviews with Australian artists confirmed these are not isolated examples. The respondents who had experience with major labels echoed the suggestion that musicians themselves do not typically fare well from the star system. Most responded on the condition of anonymity, and many were unimpressed by their personal relationships with the recording industry. One told the story of how a particular radio station was happy to take money to advertise his album on the air, but explained that his music could not possibly be part of their playlist, which consisted entirely of classic hits from the twentieth century. Another suggested that despite being involved in a song that reached the Top Ten internationally, he had never seen a cent from the record company. A jazz musician bemoaned the fact that niche genres were paid scant attention by the labels.

A member of one of Australia's most successful bands from the 1980s suggested that the record companies had been "exploiting people for a long, long time. The whole relationship between record companies and radio is completely corrupt." Artists with intimate experience of the industry displayed resentment towards some labels' make-or-break approach to music: "There's no development anymore. In the 70s and 80s you'd get three or five album deals. Now you get one and if that doesn't work, you're gone." Interestingly, experienced musicians (including some established household names) were the most vocal in suggesting that the old model was dead – and good riddance:

"They were ripping us off. We sold 250,000 records and didn't make a penny." Many embraced the new technologies and services as a way of reclaiming control: "Our new trio will bypass record companies and use MySpace."

However, not all interviewees were negative. When quizzed about the recording industry, some younger bands considered that success was only achievable by signing with a major label: "We're still trying to get signed by a record company … the only ones making it are on labels." One interviewee (most likely echoing the truth of the matter) expressed that she wanted "to be played on radio" and that signing with a label would make that a reality. Others considered signing with a major label the final and ultimate step in a musical career: "I'll probably take the indie path to start, but probably want to get signed eventually."

The interviewees provided a range of responses, but all alluded to a period of transition – and expanded opportunity. The major labels still wield significant market power, whilst alternative publicity, marketing and distribution models are still in flux. Arguably, the reach and clout of the major labels is still required to create global stars on a par with Justin Bieber or Lady Gaga. However, it is possible to make a living as a musician by taking advantage of new media technologies. In many instances, the star system has been more of a boon to the record labels than the artists themselves.

For independents, the ability to connect with fans and offer them unique and scarce goods (often not the music tracks themselves) provides a mechanism for an alternative music industry approach. It may not replace the majors, but it can exist in parallel, providing an outlet for those musicians and fans wishing to participate. Brian Austin Whitney, founder of Just Plain Folks, proposed the 5000 Fans Theory: any artist with 5000 fans (each willing to spend $20 per annum on CDs, download, merchandise and gigs) can stand to earn $100,000 a year. Kevin Kelly's 1000 True Fans meme (2008b) argues the same point:

> A creator, such [as] an artist, musician, photographer, craftsperson, performer, animator, designer, videomaker, or author – in other words, anyone producing works of art – needs to acquire only 1,000 True Fans to make a living.

> A True Fan is defined as someone who will purchase anything and everything you produce. They will drive 200 miles to see you sing. They will buy the super deluxe re-issued hi-res box set of your stuff even though they have the low-res version. They have a Google Alert set for your name. They bookmark the eBay page where your out-of-print editions show up. They come to your openings. They have you sign their copies. They buy the t-shirt, and the mug, and the hat. They can't wait till you issue your next work. They are true fans.

Both ideas are attractive because the number of fans, whilst not insignificant, is low enough to be seen as achievable. Although gaining 1000 or 5000 fans through selling CDs at the local pub would be extremely difficult, the internet's global reach has shifted the potential to meet that imagined quota for success. It might be difficult to secure 1000 hardcore thrash metal fans in suburban Sydney, but it would surely be possible to find ten fans in each of 100 towns around the world.

Whitney and Kelly's approaches reflect Chris Anderson's notion of the long tail, which suggests that given the visibility and availability that the internet allows, a plethora of viable niches can exist in any market. We noted in the last chapter that the shape of music sales has undergone a significant shift; the first decade of the twenty-first century saw a dramatic drop in sales compared to the heady peaks of the 1980s. As a consequence Anderson (2006: 32–3) argues that the hit album has been mortally wounded as more music floods into the online market. No longer constrained by limited availability in bricks-and-mortar stores, the diversity of accessible music has reshaped our engagement. Our consumption is no longer restricted to a small number of blockbuster hits; we are listening to the long tail – a wider range of smaller-selling artists. Anderson (2006: 35) asks,

> What if there were 400 Top 40s, one for each narrow music niche? Or 40,000? Or 400,000? Suddenly the concept of the hit gives way to the micro-hit. The singular star is joined by a swarm of micro-stars, and a tiny number of mass-market elites become an unlimited number of niche demi-elites. The population of "hits" grows hugely, each one with smaller but presumably more engaged audiences.

Of course, the long-tail theory has given rise to some objections (Elberse 2008: 88–96), but irrespective of the theoretical debate about its overall impact, it does accurately describe the scenario within which individual musicians – as well as other content creators – find themselves. The increased accessibility afforded by the internet has increased the availability of products, placing a global cottage industry of production, marketing and distribution *alongside* the twentieth-century blockbuster approach.

The Cult of the Professional

A key oppositional response to the emergence of a greater range of music has been the idea that the increase in quantity comes at the expense of quality; that whilst the industrial model of the major corporations may have diminished the number of musicians to which we were exposed, it ensured that resources (from both a producer and a consumer perspective) were not wasted on unworthy artists. For example, Andrew Keen doubts that emerging internet-based business models are sustainable. His primary objections centre on production from outside a centrally controlled (or monopolistic) industry that traditionally has been the arbiter of quality and reliability. Keen rejects much of the more interesting emerging media products simply because they have been produced and distributed using an alternative industrial process and argues that there is no evidence that those alternative processes are viable. When Keen was writing *The Cult of the Amateur* in 2006, a Seattle band, the Scene Aesthetic, had notched up over 9 million song plays on MySpace and half a million views on YouTube. Quick to point out that the band had still to make these statistics translate into dollars, Keen overlooked two important factors. First, the Scene Aesthetic's social media presence fostered a direct line of communication with the audience, which had the potential to transform some listeners into paying gig-goers. Second, snapshots of the internet are just that – snapshots. And the picture from subsequent snapshots has a habit of changing over time. By October 2011, the Scene Aesthetic had a significant online store on the Mischief Market selling music and merchandise, as well as offerings via the usual suspects such as iTunes and Amazon. Five years on from Keen's critique, they have not yet signed with a major label, but they are still around, still making music, still touring (nationally and overseas) and – well – succeeding. In any other era, it is unlikely that this level of success could have been achieved, but in the twenty-first century, through the affordances of the network, the Scene Aesthetic and countless other bands continue to maintain a global presence.

Importantly, despite Keen's arguments to the contrary, the continuing existence of such independent musicians has not been at the expense of musicians curated by major labels. Adele still wins Grammys and sells millions of songs, despite the presence of alternative approaches to monetizing music. Keen's "cult of the amateur" has not killed the mass market for music, but instead has provided opportunities for other approaches to be viable.

Arguably, the traditional music industry has itself been problematic. This cult of the professional has never rewarded individuals according to pure talent – indeed, there are cases where extraordinary music has languished due to the lack of major label attention. Understandably, the motivations of major labels tend towards potential profit and (notwithstanding arguments over what the terms quality and talent actually mean) the star system tends to be conservative and promote music and musicians that have already been proven in the marketplace. Experimenting with innovation is a risk that runs counter to this, and as a result, many musicians have been unable find a place with a major label. Excluded from the system, they have struggled to find an outlet, or a way to make an "agreeable living". Until recently.

'It's the End of the World as I Know It (and I Feel Fine)'

The internet represents a possible salvation from total obscurity, a mechanism to bypass the traditional pathway to musical success. One prominent example is Jonathan Coulton. A former programmer turned musician, he decided in September 2006 to release a new song every week for a year; all of them were made available under a Creative Commons licence authorizing consumers to freely share the track. He achieved a modicum of fame when his song 'Code Monkey' (2006) was picked up by the popular geek blog Slashdot; Coulton's songs were shared widely and he leveraged his popularity to earn an income from performing live shows. Contrary to the "peanuts" that Keen (2007: 31) claims are on offer in such models of production, Coulton was somewhat embarrassed to reveal that he earned close to half a million dollars in 2010 from paid downloads and other music-related activities.

Coulton's approach to music is undeniably niche, and exemplifies the opportunities that the new technologies afford. But there remains a scepticism that his approach represents a viable future. In discussion with Alex Blumberg for an NPR Planet Money podcast in May 2011, Jacob Ganz and Frannie Kelley from NPR Music emphasized the freakish nature of his success. The interview centred on the question, "Is Coulton a fluke, or is he a new model of how to make a living as a musician?" (Blumberg 2011) and the programme concluded that the former was true, dismissing the idea that it was viable for other musicians to capitalize on niche audiences. Responding via his blog, Coulton (2011) argued that Ganz and Kelley had missed the point. To him, success in the music industry had always involved the lucky break and he had won the so-called internet lottery just as the Beatles had done with the "British Invasion". He went on:

> And that is the point. That is what's inarguably different today because of the internet. We now have an entirely new set of contexts and they come with a whole new set of tools that give us cheap and easy access to all of them – niche has gone mainstream. It is no longer necessary to organize your business or your art around geography, or storage space, or capital, or what's cool in your town, or any other physical constraint. And this is not to say that anyone can become a moderately successful rockstar just by starting a blog – success is still going to be a rare and miraculous thing, as it has always been. There are just a lot more ways to get there than there used to be, and people are finding new ones every day.

Coulton echoes a shift in mindset that is becoming more commonplace amongst music communities. For the most part, musicians had aspired to sign major label contracts and sell millions of albums and singles. Whilst that remains a dream for many, the internet has enabled many others to succeed on different terms. Coulton explains:

> I obviously don't know the details of everyone's business, but I'm guessing that we have this one thing in common: we've all decided that it's fine with us if we reach fewer people as long as we reach them more directly. The revolution in the music industry (which has already happened by the way) is one of efficiency, and it means that success is now possible on a much smaller scale. Nobody has to sell out Madison Square Garden anymore to make a living.

So, is Coulton a fluke? Or can his success be replicated? Certainly there are other artists with similar success stories. As Everett Reed (2004: 52) suggests, "Everybody wants to be a star, and doing an audience participation number helps a lucky few." Boston singer Matthew Ebel (http://matthewebel.com) is another artist who understands this principle. Leveraging social networks and virtual spaces, Ebel's online biography recounts how he regularly performed as "a piano-banging bird named *Hali Heron*" in the online virtual world Second Life before his audience outgrew the number that the virtual world could accommodate. Ebel's shtick is an innovative subscription system that forges intimate connections with his fans; as his website reads "This is not Matthew Ebel's website … it's yours." The site offers a tiered system of subscriptions ranging from $4.99 to $14.99 per month, and each package offers an increasing amount of value-added material and access that embody principles found in Kelly's "generatives", eight uncopiable values (2008a). Kelly suggests that when copies are superabundant they become worthless, and the following factors provide scarcity and therefore value: immediacy, personalization, interpretation, authenticity, accessibility, embodiment, patronage and findability. He notes,

> These eight qualities require a new skill set. Success in the free-copy world is not derived from the skills of distribution since the Great Copy Machine in the Sky takes care of that. Nor are legal skills surrounding Intellectual Property and Copyright very useful anymore. Nor are the skills of hoarding and scarcity. Rather, these new eight generatives demand an understanding of how abundance breeds a sharing mindset, how generosity is a business model, how vital it has become to cultivate and nurture qualities that can't be replicated with a click of the mouse.

Ebel's subscription packages include offerings such as live concert recordings, discounts in Ebel's online store, members-only "rehearse-o-cam" and executive producer credits on new releases. According to a feature in *Techdirt*, Ebel had generated enough money to make music his full-time job, with revenue from subscriptions representing about 40 per cent of his overall income (Masnick 2010).

The personal touch appears to be one particular area for innovation in audience engagement and Ebel is not alone in experimenting with its possibilities. One of our interviewees sold CDs direct from her website with the added bonus that purchasing more than twenty copies in one transaction came with a free twenty-minute live performance at the buyer's home: "We sold 10,000 copies and did over 100 of those parties. Not bad for an independent record with no radio airplay." A more unusual example is found in Moldover, a San Francisco-based musician and exponent of controllerism – the art and science of using MIDI controllers to create and perform music. His approach was to develop and distribute an album with a unique physicality. The CD case is a working circuit board that functions as a musical instrument. (See http://www.youtube.com/watch?v=T8UzSVFUIc0 for a demonstration.) Pressing a button on the case triggers a noise that can be modified by light sensors; its sound can be output via an onboard 3.5-mm socket. Sales of the $34 CD were strong – distributed, of course, directly through Moldover's website. One viewer of the demo video on YouTube commented "This seriously turned me from pirating the album to actually buying it. Damn, that's how you do it."

With or Without You?

Andrew Keen (2007: 33) does not deny that the internet allows the emergence of niche markets, but argues, "The more specialized the niche, the narrower the market. The narrower the market, the more shoestring the production budget, which compromises the quality." Again, Keen overlooks some pertinent factors (and his argument may be more applicable to cultural products which demand high budgets, such as Hollywood action movies). The affordances of the personal computer and affordable DAW software mean that high production values *can* occur on a shoestring budget. The long tail does not necessitate a lack of quality in the music that is produced. Keen expresses an anxiety that record companies

> are struggling just to survive, we're pumping all our money instead into businesses that offer nothing more than infinite advertising space in exchange for user-generated nonsense that couldn't be published or distributed through any professional source. (2007: 138)

Whilst there may well be examples of what Keen suggests, he underestimates the average fan. If fans' embrace of niche musical acts is at the expense of "professionally" produced music from the major labels, then something is clearly amiss with how those major labels are selecting, producing or marketing their music; ostensibly this is unlikely, considering that the majors have far more experience in this area than a niche act releasing its debut album. To offer a simple counter to Keen's naysaying, we suggest that this exemplifies the disintermediation and reintermediation that we have previously discussed; that is not to say that alternative music strategies are not without their challenges and limitations.

Chris Anderson (2006: 105) offers up the San Francisco band Birdmonster as an example of reintermediation. In addition to digital distribution via CDBaby, Birdmonster uses the internet to locate gigs, touting its social media presence to prove it can draw a crowd. The band's relative success led to offers from managers, labels and traditional industry folks but all were rejected because in the band-members' words "It didn't add up". In Anderson's analysis a record label

> exists to primarily fulfill four functions: (1) talent scouting; (2) financing (the advances bands get to pay for their studio time is like seed capital invested by a venture capitalist); (3) distribution; and (4) marketing. (2006, 106)

Signing to a label "didn't add up" for Birdmonster because for minimal cost it had managed to fulfil all these functions and maintain control; recording costs were absorbed directly by the band members (and their credit cards). New intermediaries such as CDBaby handled distribution and social media was leveraged for marketing.

In the reintermediated music ecology the label has been displaced by a combination of new intermediaries capable of distributing songs to the top tier of retailers and marketing direct to Twitter and Facebook feeds. There are, however, challenges and limitations to this approach. In the absence of a label and manager the labour of promoting and arranging releases and distribution falls on the band's shoulders. As of October 2011 Birdmonster had signed to indie label The FADER (who also handled the physical release of Saul Williams's *The Inevitable Rise And Liberation Of Niggy Tardust!* (2007) seven months after its digital release), but the pathways have clearly changed.

As we explored in earlier chapters, the options available to artists have expanded dramatically. Signing to a major label is only one possibility – a number of alternative intermediaries have emerged, and the internet has, for some musicians, removed altogether the need for an intermediary. Indeed, the parameters of the industry have undoubtedly shifted, the key difference being that the gatekeepers – whilst not totally removed – have been displaced. The marketplace for musicians is a far more accessible place. Success in that market still requires talent, persistence and sheer luck, but at least any musician can now set up a stall in the bazaar. Moreover, the possibilities in the bazaar continue to expand; creative musicians are finding new ways to leverage the possibilities of the internet.

New Connections

When we conducted our interviews and survey of Australian musicians some key themes emerged. It would be inappropriate to draw singular conclusions from such a diverse group of musicians, but there was striking similarity in many opinions expressed. There was a common understanding amongst musicians that times were changing – that the recording industry was in a state of flux as new intermediaries (at the time of the research) such as MySpace and iTunes offered new forms of engagement and distribution. Most artists were aware that the new technologies allowed for direct engagement with their audiences particularly through social media, and many had grasped the opportunities with both hands. Similarly, many had thoroughly embraced digital distribution, leading to a general sense that record labels were less important. There was a common scepticism about labels, which tended to revolve around two factors. First, that online tools and platforms replaced the functions of record companies and, second, a more general cynicism that they were "big, slow-moving beasts" that had "dropped the ball" by being the last to the digital party. That said, younger musicians tended to retain an aspiration to get signed, arguably because of their lack of experience with the twentieth-century business model. A number of respondents pointed to the shift away from hierarchical modes towards a mesh-like or networked approach in which various actors and nodes connected through websites, services and widgets where – to echo Kevin Kelly (2005: 4) – "every link is both a point of departure and destination".

The connectivity of networks allowed musicians to establish a new kind of economic relationship with fans. Whilst social networking did not directly generate sales in terms of CDs or downloads, many of our interview respondents indicated that it was the most potent in an artist's arsenal of promotional tools. There was a consensus that networking helps convert ephemeral notions such as interest and discoverability into attendance at gigs, where further connections can be forged and income generated, through selling CDs and merchandise. Although interviewees frequently stated that live performance was a generator of revenue and driver for sales of recordings there was an acknowledgement that "performing live is also a hard way to make money. Touring is expensive." Some of our respondents also found selling music online to be problematic. At the time of the interview, the Australian iTunes store had only been in operation for two years and many found it was a far from frictionless tool. One respondent cited the reams of legal paperwork (which he felt unqualified to assess) as a barrier to entry, exacerbated by different requirements for the various international stores: "The paperwork for international stores is overwhelming." Others complained about the amount of time taken to process applications, suggesting that – for the Australian store at least – there were insufficient staff for efficiency. Some opted to set up online stores on their own websites using existing services like PayPal to handle financial transactions. As pointed out previously, many of the issues raised by interviewees have since become less of an obstacle with intermediaries such as TuneCore and CDBaby functioning as agents to negotiate these hurdles on behalf of artists for a small fee.

Whilst not always translating into direct economic opportunities, network connections can lead to sales. One metal band from Sydney reported how it had received unsolicited interest via MySpace from a German record label that wanted to release a couple of songs as singles. Another, a classical composer, established a contact via MySpace that resulted in a commission for a piece of work to be performed at the Lincoln Center in New York. The impression gained from the interviews was that MySpace "is a good marketing tool"; whilst several interviewees reported they were not making money directly through digital distribution, social networking allowed for the establishment of a "digital business card", which could lead to collaborative endeavours such as remixing projects and shared gigs or draw record-label interest.

Indeed, the key currency of social networking may be attention. The Gregory Brothers (a New York band perhaps best known for their series of "Autotune the News" videos) provide an example. The videos took footage from news broadcasts featuring politicians, anchors, pundits and witnesses and "songified" them using the auto-tune audio effect that was brought into popular consciousness by Cher's 'Believe' (1998) and numerous tracks by T-Pain. 'Bed Intruder Song' has been viewed over 100 million times on YouTube and evolved into an iTunes single. Another track, 'Backin Up Song' (2010) took interview footage from local news coverage of a convenience store robbery and "songified" it, also resulting in millions of views on YouTube and another iTunes release. (The revenue from iTunes sales is split between the Gregory Brothers and Diana Radcliffe, whose witness testimony to the robbery provides the vocals.) That song's story does not end there, though. It was covered by Walk off the Earth, a Canadian indie band, who performed an acoustic ska version, which itself became a YouTube and iTunes hit. Walk off the Earth (WOTE) also achieved fame with a YouTube cover of Gotye's 'Somebody That I Used To

Know' performed by all five band members on a single guitar. WOTE's cover has received over 130 million views; Gotye's official video of his original has about double that number. Goyte himself, a Belgian-born Australian musician, built his career with self-published CDs before breaking out on the national public broadcaster's youth network. This web of connections between musicians and their music is a feature of the new media technologies. It is clear here that the network underlies a music ecosystem that creates new opportunities for discovery for both musicians and audiences. Whilst such possibilities may have occurred in the past, the scale, scope and sheer accessibility of music in today's media-scape is very different from the world of only three decades ago that was the sole domain of the chart-driven blockbuster.

Writing Their Own Story of Success

The interviews with Australian musicians were conducted in 2007 and the authors concede that things have since changed: Facebook has largely replaced MySpace. Intermediaries like TuneCore drastically reduce the logistical burden of digital distribution. iTunes has become the largest music retailer in the world and a host of other platforms, communities and tools have arisen to join the twenty-first-century music ecology. Returning to the 2011 interview about Jonathan Coulton on NPR, the question of whether Coulton is a fluke or if his success can be replicated is ostensibly superfluous. This chapter has identified some high-profile success stories and revealed that musicians themselves have a changing attitude towards the industry – and notions of success. In the light of the experiences detailed above, it would have been more appropriate and perhaps pressing for NPR to kick-start a cascade of other more pertinent questions concerning the new music ecology – questions that failed to be asked during the interview but which Coulton himself raised in his blogged response:

> How much money is actually being made in this space that never gets tracked as part of the music industry? What percentage of full time professional artists are making a living, and how does that compare to the old record biz? … is filesharing/piracy hurting artists, or just labels (or is it hurting anyone)? (Coulton 2011)

Although we do not have the complete answers to those questions, we would suggest that there is an existent middle class of musicians that is often overshadowed by individual stories of success that are typically written off as gimmicky or flukes. As we have argued throughout this book, the media space has changed dramatically and as a result we should not expect the twentieth-century model to continue as the status quo. What is more, as the ecology shifts and evolves the beneficiaries may also change. The new technologies afforded by the network empower artists previously locked out of the twentieth-century business model to find audiences, generate income and achieve success.

In his keynote speech at the 2008 GRAMMY Northwest MusicTech Summit Ian Rogers (CEO of Topspin Media) offered the opinion that the only perspectives that matter are those of the artist and the fan. From his considerable experience with the music industry, Rogers argued that the new music ecology gives artists "an ability to take their careers into their own hands, to redefine what success means for them" (Topspin 2008). Though securing a label contract remains the ultimate ambition for many artists, there are many more revelling in having choices for their music and their careers – choices that did not exist a decade ago:

> Instead of doing a 360 deal with a label artists are able to do a 360 deal with themselves and choose their business partners based on who is going to add the most value.

The choices now available to musicians of every level redefine the state of play; the twentieth-century model is mitigated by a plethora of alternative routes that empower artists, allowing them to retain ownership of their recordings and exploit them as they see fit.

That ownership speaks to the next key element of the Music 2.0 discourse – the divide between authorship and ownership in the recording industry. Whilst the RIAA habitually argues that digitally sharing music harms musicians, the fact remains that in a typical record deal artists assign the copyright in recordings to the record label and only receive royalties. As bands such as Def Leppard and Radiohead have pointed out, disputes can occur over royalties and in some older contracts, royalties are not paid at all for digital sales. In that context, musicians have an interest in adopting new platforms and approaches for releasing music, which can circumvent the traditional arrangements and allow them to retain the copyrights in their music. Some, like David Bowie, believe that copyright is an obsolete notion, pronouncing in 2002 that "I'm fully confident that copyright, for instance, will no longer exist in 10 years, and authorship and intellectual property is in for such a bashing" (Pareles 2002: 2). More than ten years later and Bowie's confidence is proved misplaced; copyright is still with us and the authors do not expect that to change any time soon. But, clearly, artists are taking the opportunity to make better use of the rights they do have and the new technologies have enabled them to retain more control. Intriguingly, these opportunities have coincided with a previously obscure provision in US copyright law which takes effect from 2013. This "termination rights" clause allows artists to recover (from their record labels) the rights for songs and recordings licensed 35 years ago. So, just as the new music ecology is enabling musicians to bypass the need to license their copyrights to major labels, for the sake of mass-market publishing and distribution, those same labels may be losing the legal rights that allowed them to build their twentieth-century businesses. The next chapter explores what this might mean.

7 Shaking the Foundations

Legend has it that Robert Johnson sold his soul to the devil in exchange for the blues-playing talent for which he is famous. However plausible that legend may be (he was, after all, also a member of the mythical "27 club", having been found dead in a Mississippi hotel room at that relatively tender age), the reality is that his musical career has been far more lucrative post-mortem. Indeed, due to the convoluted development of US legislation, copyright in his small but influential body of blues remains in the control of his estate until 2047 – well over a hundred years after his death in relative poverty. Clearly copyright laws played little part in provoking Johnson's music creativity. Just as clearly, copyright has ensured that his creativity continues to benefit a select few – in this case, his estate and those his estate has chosen to do business with – at the expense of continuing the blues conversation of which his music is so much a part.

The Johnson example illustrates the (dis)connection between copyright, musicians and the music business. As Steve Gordon, author of *The Future of the Music Business* states, "Copyright is the house in which the music business lives, and without it the business would be homeless and broke" (2005: 3). This is not hyperbole; the music publishing and recording industries are dependent on acquiring and exploiting copyrights – and musicians typically sign away their various performing and publishing rights in return for recording contracts. This separation of authorship and ownership has been a feature of distribution models since the early days of the print industry – but as we have discussed in this book, musicians are able, through the new media technologies, to take advantage of different opportunities. Reclaiming their rights is one of those opportunities.

This chapter looks briefly at the history of copyright, traces some affordances presented by the new media technologies, and explores how those affordances might be exploited within the evolving copyright realm.

Of Authors and Owners

Copyright, in any form vaguely resembling our contemporary laws, emerged in early-eighteenth-century England. The world's first piece of copyright legislation was the Statute of Anne (1710) – its long title being *An Act for the Encouragement of Learning, by vesting the Copies of Printed Books in the Authors or purchasers of such Copies, during the Times therein mentioned.* Designed to provide an incentive to create works that would inform and advance society (hence its title), the law secured literary copyrights for authors. But in the centuries since its introduction, copyright law has been reconfigured by particular interests and reshaped at the provocation of new technologies. The very idea behind its existence has been twisted to ensure that rights have been extended in both scope and duration.

Although the Statute of Anne might have been the first copyright law, trade regulation and numerous other forms of legal protection preceded it. A group of London-based book printers called the Stationers' Company operated a de facto monopoly over the printing of books. Largely protected by a Crown Charter issued in 1553, the Stationers purchased manuscripts outright from authors, who were paid a fee and no ongoing royalties. Trade practice treated ownership of books as a property right – inviolable and perpetual. Ownership was entered into a register; Crown support and internal trade regulation meant that only registered works could be printed. The separation of authorship and ownership was the backbone of the print trade, as well as setting a template for the content industries that would later emerge.

When the Statute of Anne was introduced it awarded a copyright to authors – a limited monopoly of 14 years for new texts (and 21 years for those already in print). After 14 years the copyright would revert back to the author (if still alive) whereupon he could negotiate another publishing arrangement and attract a second bout of 14 years. Once the second period of protection expired, the text would fall into the public domain bereft of an owner, allowing anyone to make copies. This limited monopoly ensured that authors could profit from their work, but provided an incentive to keep creating new texts. Initially, the Statute of Anne was ignored and the Stationers kept to business as usual. It was simply not their trade practice to revert ownership back to the author (Donaldson v. Becket 1774: 1086), and the registration system perpetuated the Stationers' control over publishing.

In 1731, things changed: the first statutory copyrights expired for works that had been already in print when the 1710 Act came into force. Commercially important works by Shakespeare, Milton and Locke (amongst others) fell into the public domain. Feather (1988: 378) reports that works by these authors formed the "cornerstone of the whole book trade, and the trade feared it would be ruined if these copies were no longer protected". That same year, the Stationers petitioned Parliament for stronger protection and positioned themselves as simple agents working for the benefit of authors. A parliamentary committee was informed of "29 authors, who had had their works pirated, and then some living examples were paraded in front of them"

(Feather 1994: 71). New protection was granted and the import of cheap reprints was banned in an effort to force the domestic market to depend on the London-based industry. However, as current experience has demonstrated, legislation does not halt piracy and the lack of impact was no different in the eighteenth century. Being London-based, the Stationers had difficulty supplying the north of the country; pirate Scottish printers were happy to pick up the slack. The English printers attempted an array of solutions including petitioning for more legislative protection, ignoring the activities in the north and even pooling all their resources to purchase all Scottish reprints to remove them from general circulation. None of these efforts were particularly successful and that contested nature of copyright remains to this day. Whilst we have glossed over many details of the eighteenth-century literary property debate, three characteristics of that contest are still identifiable today. First, modern content industries are not that different from their eighteenth-century ancestors and there remains a distinct separation of authorship and ownership. Copyrights may initially vest in "authors" (in this context used as a generic term referring to all kinds of creative types), but it is typical practice for those rights to be assigned to a gatekeeper such as a publisher or recording label. Second, copyright is contingent on policy decisions; if the Stationers (or their contemporary counterparts) wanted stronger rights, then all they had to do was get the law changed. Third, copyright typically worked for the benefit of the Stationers, but authors were tactically deployed to generate sympathy for petitions for stronger protection. Evidently, whilst the specific stakeholders in the copyright contest may have changed over the centuries, that contest remains eerily similar.

Music Copyright

Music copyright is a complex area and a single song can attract numerous different rights held by several different individuals and/or companies. A full discussion of music copyright is beyond the scope of this book, but Steve Gordon's *The Future of the Music Business* provides a comprehensive overview (2005). At the most basic level, a recording will involve at least two forms of copyright – one in the song itself and one in the recording – and a number of uses are attached to each. For example, the US Copyright Act 1976, section 106, gives copyright owners a bundle of exclusive rights in the production of copies (of sheet music or recordings), public performance (radio play, cover versions) and derivative works (remixes, mash-ups). Copyrights in music start with the artist but are frequently transferred to other parties: songwriters often assign their rights to publishers in exchange for advance payment, proffering songs to recording artists or collecting songwriting royalties. Musicians and bands assign their sound recording rights to labels for similar reasons; it becomes a necessary evil to receive advances, distribution and promotion. Once the copyrights are transferred, the artist receives royalty payments, usually somewhere between 10 and 20 per cent.

This arrangement, while traditional, is not without its critics: "Love's Manifesto" (Love 2001) and "The Problem with Music" (Albini 1994) address exploitative, yet standard, industry practices. Brereton (2009), Hall (2002) and Hervey (2002: 286–9) specifically address unconscionable contractual practices. The separation of authorship and ownership leaves many musicians stripped of any rights in their recordings, but this standard industry practice has been a necessary trade-off for many – major recording labels offer the means to reach an audience and gain fame or fortune. The label expands its portfolio and is able to exploit the recordings through single and album sales, as well as licensing opportunities with films, television shows, advertisements and videogames. "The values of [recording] companies are determined by assets, and those assets are the ownership of master recordings," points out Ron Stone, manager for Bonnie Raitt and Tracey Chapman (Boehlert 2000: 3).

Roberts (2002: 25) attributes an estimated 90 per cent of the recorded music market to the major labels. An alternative figure is provided through utilizing the Herfindahl-Hirschman Index (HII). The HII is "calculated by summing the squares of the percentage market shares held by participating firms" and "provides a measure of an industry's concentration" (Maul 2004: 365). Fagin *et al.* calculate that the major labels occupy 82 per cent of the total market for recorded music (2002: 535, n.370). Although these figures are over a decade old and may omit the middle class of musician we argued for in the previous chapter, the numbers illustrate the sheer size of an industry dependent on copyrights. Much like the Stationers' Company, the business practices of the twentieth-century record labels are implicitly tied to the regulated ownership of commodified artefacts. Wikström (2009: 21) reminds us that "Only very few are able to actually *own* music, since full and exclusive copyright of a single commercially successful song is most likely far beyond the financial constraints of the average consumer" and that when a CD is purchased the only right granted is that "to listen to the sound recording within certain carefully defined restrictions".

The strict regulation of ownership (and its separation from authorship) has even put record labels at odds with the artists who produced the music. In 1998 Public Enemy uploaded mp3s of *Bring The Noise 2000* to its website before Def Jam had released it. PolyGram (Def Jam's parent company) ordered the removal of the files (Freund 1999). The Beastie Boys echoed Public Enemy's actions and suffered a similar response from their record label, Capitol Records. The following year Tom Petty uploaded 'Free Girl Now' to MP3.com to the chagrin of Warner Bros., which immediately ordered its removal (*Billboard*, 1999: 75). More recently, alternative/industrial hip-hop outfit Death Grips earned the enmity of their record label Epic by releasing *NO LOVE DEEP WEB* for free via their website before the masters had been delivered to Epic and without the label's knowledge, let alone consent. Consequently, Epic had the content pulled from the internet before terminating its contract with Death Grips (Pelly 2012).

Digital technologies proved to be something of a tipping point for an industry keen on maintaining the profitability of those rights. Traditionally, the difficulty of copying materials provided some measure of protection for copyright owners; accessible, perfect copies were a consequence of the increasing penetration of digital computers, further exacerbated by the distribution potential of the internet. Ironically, it was the record companies' format shift to the digital CD (a move that the more cynical saw as a ploy to force consumers to re-purchase music they already owned) that enabled the ease of copying. By providing music as digital files, the industry fell foul of a generation empowered by unprecedented computing and communications technologies. There are an enormous number of unauthorized music files constantly distributed across the internet, and this quantum shift to digital has for some (Kelly 2008; Anderson 2006) fundamentally altered all media markets. The value of music in the twentieth century was linked to its relative scarcity – and the ability of the industry to control that scarcity. That scarcity is not a natural part of the digital media environment. Indeed, the new "nature" is one in which users have become accustomed to taking advantage of the possible, as opposed to the legal – ignoring any artificial scarcity manufactured by the business.

Just as the Stationers did two hundred years ago, the explosion in digital piracy led the RIAA and its international counterparts to lobby for stronger legislative protection, introduce DRM-encumbered audio files and launch anti-piracy campaigns aimed at deterrence and education. The industry's desire for self-preservation is reflected in continual calls for expanded copyrights – longer protection periods and stronger anti-piracy sanctions – and these calls frequently employ artists as the sympathetic face of an industry claiming ruin. In one such campaign, Britney Spears asked, "Would you go into a CD store and steal a CD? It's the same thing – people going into the computers and logging on and stealing our music" (Music United 2001).

The lobbying has been largely successful (at least politically) with governments altering copyright laws to support existing industries. For example, the American Digital Millennium Copyright Act 1998, the UK Digital Economy Act 2010, Australia's Digital Agenda Act 2000 and the European Union's 2011 extension of the copyright term for sound recordings all provided frameworks which enabled music (and other copyright) industries to continue with business as usual. But governments also acknowledged cultural change and the realities of the new technological context, with many legislative responses allowing some increases in time- and format-shifting for personal use, thus enshrining in law some types of practice that are in common use.

As the owners of music copyrights, record labels have never been shy to exploit their catalogues either through offering old recordings in new media formats or repackaging existing content. For example, many consumers repurchased their vinyl and cassette albums on CD (as mentioned earlier). When a new digital format – mp3 – emerged from outside the recording industry and was widely propagated by the fans themselves, the industry was slow to react. Its established grip on the chain of supply and demand was diminished and it was only by belatedly developing relationships with the new intermediaries (Apple, Amazon, Spotify *et al.*) that they were able to monetize this newly created consumer demand. Of course, those "legitimate" outlets for digital music have not replaced the "pirate" file-sharing sites, but they have provided a legal source for some. Interestingly, it appears that new releases are commonly distributed via file-sharing, with "record labels disproportionately dependent on sales of older recordings in their catalogs" (Rohter 2011). Digital sales of back catalogues rose by 12 per cent in 2010 (Browne 2011). In 2011, album sales increased 7 per cent because of a renewed interest in back catalogue. Additionally, this increase offset a 4 per cent drop in the sales for newly released albums. In the first half of 2011, 47 per cent of all albums and 60 per cent of individual tracks sold were "legacy sales" from the back catalogues of major labels (Gordon 2011).[1]

Whilst reliance on and repackaging of the back catalogue is not a new phenomenon, it has strained relationships with some artists. In November 2011, Elvis Costello advised his fans not to purchase *The Return Of The Spectacular Spinning Songbook*. Although he admired the concept and execution of the multiformat (CD, DVD, vinyl) release, Costello was dismayed by its price of over US$300, and on his blog said, "Unfortunately, we at www.elviscostello.com find ourselves unable to recommend this lovely item to you as the price appears to be either a misprint or a satire."[2]

A few months earlier, Welsh opera singer Katherine Jenkins – angry at her former record label Universal for releasing another compilation – tweeted:

---

1. http://www.digitalmusicnews.com/stories/082910termination and http://www.billboard.com/biz/articles/news/1177733/business-matters-napster-co-founder-sean-parker-now-believes-in-record
2. http://music.yahoo.com/blogs/amplifier/elvis-costello-urges-fans-avoid-200-box-set-185923124.html

> Just heard that Universal @DeccaRecords are putting out YET
> ANOTHER compilation album of my music called One Fine Day.
> Considering that I haven't recorded 4them since 2008, there is NO
> new music & it's stuff u already have. Don't want u 2 feel conned. Pls
> RT #DontBuyOneFineDay.

In July that year, Trent Reznor advised, "NIN fans, don't waste your money on this version of PHM [*Pretty Hate Machine*] that was just released ... A record label bullshit move repackaging the old album. Ignore please ...".

These are just a few examples of how copyright regimes can exacerbate the disconnection between artists and their music. Sometimes the courts can get involved, as was the case when John Fogerty was sued for copyright infringement by Fantasy, his old record label.[3] In that example, Fogerty wrote the song 'Run Through The Jungle' and assigned its copyright to Fantasy as part of a 1970 record deal with his band Creedence Clearwater Revival. Nearly fifteen years later, as a solo artist, Fogerty assigned copyright to 'The Old Man Down The Road' to Warner, his new label. Fantasy sued, claiming copyright infringement based on similarities between the two songs. Whilst Fantasy won on some claims, it lost the copyright case as the judge ruled that an artist could not plagiarize himself. Reliance on back catalogue has left the major labels in a precarious "eggs in one basket" position; what happens when ownership of the back catalogue becomes contested?

Terminator 2.0 Judgement Day?

A further example of the twists and turns of copyright can be found in termination rights. The Copyright Act 1976 is the "product of a copyright reform process that was initiated in the late 1950s" (Samuelson 2007: 553) and (subject to various amendments) is the governing force of copyright law in the USA. The Act grants exclusive and assignable intellectual property rights in creative works for the duration of the songwriter/composer's life and the following 70 years. (For recordings, the duration of copyright is measured by the number of years from the date of release.) During this period the author may transfer his copyrights as he sees fit (*Walthal* et al *v. Corey Rusk* 1999: 484).

The US copyright law is distinctive in that it still retains a reversionary provision of sorts; section 203 of the 1976 Act provides authors with a means to terminate an assignment of copyright after 35 years. Some European countries' copyright legislation contains similar provisions, but they only become enforceable 25 years after the death of the author (Torremans and Castrillón 2012). The primary difference is that the US reversionary

---

3.   *Fantasy* v. *Fogerty* 510 US 517 (1994).

right is intended to benefit a still living author whilst European laws place the author's family and/or estate as the beneficiary of reversion. Termination is not automatic; the Act merely provides a window of opportunity and of course there are formalities involved. The onus is on the author to initiate the process and section 203 terminations are subject to a number of caveats. For example, only copyright assignments made on or after 1 January 1978 (the date that the Copyright Act 1976 came into force) are eligible; thus the first opportunity to reclaim copyrights was in 2013. Further, termination only affects copyrights under the US legal jurisdiction; copyrights in foreign territories remain unaffected. Copyrights assigned prior to 1978 may also be terminated under provisions found in section 304 of the Act, but the formalities differ slightly from those exercised under section 203, which are the focus of the following discussion. To exercise the termination right, authors must terminate assignment within a five-year period that commences at the end of the thirty-fifth year. Every year after 2013 will activate new termination rights for copyrights assigned from 1978 onwards; in 2014, assignments from 1979 can be terminated and so on.

Artists with songs from this era of the recording industry's catalogue can now start to reclaim their copyrights – and regain a connection to their music. Whilst this second bite of the apple may prompt many artists to renegotiate their contracts or move to another label, the new digital environment may provoke some to bypass labels altogether.

Copyright terminations have the potential to undermine the finances of the US recording industry. Entertainment lawyer and academic Barry Heyman (2012) speculates that works eligible under section 203 include those by "luminary artists and bands such as Billy Joel, Bob Dylan, Bob Marley and the Wailers, Bruce Springsteen, The Rolling Stones, and Tom Petty, among many others". It may be a question of *when* rather than *if* artists file to terminate copyright assignments. Rick Carnes, the president of the Songwriters Guild of America and composer of country hits popularized by Reba McEntire and Garth Brooks, states he has "had the date circled in red for 35 years, and now it's time to move" (Rohter 2011: 4). Bob Dylan, Tom Petty, Bryan Adams, Loretta Lynn, Kris Kristofferson, Tom Waits and Charlie Daniels have already filed for termination. Steve Greenburg wrote and produced 'Funky Town' (1980) for Lipps Inc. and suggests artists are ready to fight for their rights: "Thirty-five years is long enough for the majors to milk a record … It's time to give it back to the owners. Plus, it's the law." Although yet to file for termination, Don Henley agrees, "It's very simple. We created these records, we paid for them. I want to pass those things along to my children. It's part of their heritage" (Browne 2011).

Having already built a substantial reputation (thanks to record deals), a musician's brand is clearly more visible – and important – than that of labels. (Would most music fans even know the record label or publishers involved with the Eagles' *Hotel California*?) In that context, the usefulness of a major label for both ensuring continuing sales of previous releases and driving sales of future releases is questionable. There are enough examples to suggest that, for established musicians, major labels are no longer necessary. As Don Henley from the Eagles suggested in an interview with *Rolling Stone* magazine:

> Artists have several things they can do. They can re-up [*sic*] with the label and use this as leverage to renegotiate a recording agreement. They can invoke termination rights and take back their master recordings and see what they can do themselves. If they get it back, they can shop it around and see if anybody else wants it – another label or an indie label or they might market it themselves on the internet. Or artists can go back and re-record everything. (Browne 2011)

(As we mentioned in Chapter 5, Def Leppard decided to re-record their own back catalogue in order to take control of their music.) Henley goes on to say "But labels are reaping what they've sown. They've got both artists and consumers mad at them now."

Adding to the challenge for the labels is the reality that those artists currently on the verge of being able to enact their termination rights are amongst the most consistent revenue generators. That same *Rolling Stone* article suggests, "So in 2013, major labels could potentially be deprived revenue from classic 1978 albums like Bruce Springsteen's *Darkness On The Edge Of Town*, Billy Joel's *52nd Street* and Bob Dylan's *Street-Legal*."

As previously mentioned, the contribution of legacy recordings (Resnikoff 2011) to overall sales figures is significant, making the back catalogue a cornerstone of the recording industry's source of revenue. Whilst not all back catalogue titles are in the frame for termination rights, the potential exists for substantial downside for the major labels and a further undermining of the existing music industries.

The RIAA's stance is clear; Kenneth Abdo, a lawyer for the National Academy of Recording Arts and Sciences, is exercising termination rights for a number of clients including Kool and the Gang and says that the labels are clear in that "they will not relinquish recordings they consider their property without a fight". Given the profitability of the back catalogue, the similarities with 1731 are clear, and, like the Stationers, the recording industry took preemptive steps to protect its interests.

In 1999 the RIAA had the law changed. Section 203(a) states

> In the case of any work *other than a work made for hire*, the exclusive
> or nonexclusive grant of a transfer or license of copyright or of any
> right under a copyright, executed by the author on or after January
> 1, 1978, otherwise than by will, is subject to termination ....

Put simply, works made for hire cannot be terminated. The Act defines "work
made for hire" in section 101 as

> (1) a work prepared by an employee within the scope of his or her
> employment; or (2) a work specially ordered or commissioned for
> use as a contribution to a collective work, as a part of a motion pic-
> ture or other audiovisual work, as a translation, as a supplementary
> work, as a compilation, as an instructional text, as a test, as answer
> material for a test, or as an atlas, if the parties expressly agree in a
> written instrument signed by them that the work shall be consid-
> ered a work made for hire.

The second paragraph details the nine categories that can constitute a work
made for hire. Note that sound recordings are not expressly included.

In 1999, Mitch Glazier, chief counsel for the congressional copyright subcommittee, made a small amendment to this second paragraph via the (otherwise totally unconnected) Satellite Home Viewer Improvement Act 1999.
Glazier, who eventually secured employment with the RIAA, inserted the
words "as a sound recording" after "audiovisual work", reclassifying sound
recordings as works made for hire and exempt from termination under section 203. For musicians – who were not consulted – this amendment was far
from "non-controversial and technical in nature" (Boehlert 2000: 2), as Glazier
had presented it. In an arrangement where a work is made for hire, musicians
effectively become employees rather than independent authors who assign
their rights to labels; the law treats the author as though he did not participate in the creative process. Works made for hire remain protected for a fixed
term of 95 years, perhaps not as long as "life plus 70" but longer than if terminations of copyright were allowed to succeed. The Work Made for Hire and
Copyright Corrections Act 2000 quickly repealed the change at the request of
a record industry facing extensive criticism from its artists, who were levelling
accusations of underhand tactics.

Notwithstanding the fact that its attempts to change the law ultimately
failed, the RIAA still argues that sound recordings are legally classified as works
made for hire and that Glazier's amendment was merely to clarify a common
understanding within the industry. General counsel Steven Marks states, "We

believe the termination right doesn't apply to most sound recordings" (Rohter 2011: 4). As part of standard practice, major labels advance money so that artists can record and produce an album. The advance, amongst many other costs, is repaid via deductions from the royalties paid to artists when their music is sold. If the recording industry asserts continued ownership pursuant to a termination, it will create a "pay off the mortgage but still not own the house" situation for its artists. (Although it must be acknowledged that not all albums break even.) June Besek from the Columbia University School of Law further questions the RIAA's confidence that musicians are its employees:

> Where do they work? Do you pay Social Security for them? Do you withdraw taxes from a paycheck? Under those kinds of definitions it seems pretty clear that your standard kind of recording artist from the 1970s or 1980s is not an employee but an independent contractor. (Rohter 2011: 4)

The contest continues. If artists are successful in reclaiming copyrights, the loss of rights in the master recordings could deprive the labels of numerable assets of substantial value: "Just imagine, if you will, the value of masters (if they were post-1978) of The Beatles, The Beach Boys, The Rolling Stones, David Bowie, Frank Sinatra, Elvis Presley, etc., 35 years after their original delivery" (Burry and Cooper 2001: 9). Owners of reclaimed copyrights will be in a position to renegotiate contractual agreements with labels or ignore them completely and leverage the web's potential for distribution and marketing.

Conclusion – Rights Matter

The consequences of musicians enacting their termination rights over the next decade would not be so problematic for the majors if it were not for the possibilities described in this book. The intricacies of termination are (at the time of writing) still playing out (Caplan 2012) but it is a clear example of how the digital technologies have shifted the relationship between musicians and their music – and enabled the rethinking of twentieth-century approaches to assigning copyrights.

Whilst not quite the perfect storm of circumstances, the affordances of Music 2.0 have empowered musicians with options that were not available a mere decade ago. We have seen in previous chapters how established artists have the ability to use the internet to forge their own marketing and distribution channels. As well as taking their business to another label, musicians can turn to the new intermediaries, whether they be aggregators or Live Nation style promoters – or reach out to their audiences directly.

Termination rights are geographically specific and at this stage it is difficult to determine how widespread their impact will be. Notwithstanding that, they do exemplify the possibilities and provide a highly visible example for all musicians – who may choose to take control of their copyrights from day one, rather than wait until termination rights are available to them. As the broader music industry begins to come to terms with the viability of the digital context, and musicians gain a broader understanding of how rights matter, the near future in the evolution of copyright debates will prove as fascinating as the past.

8 It's the Music, Stupid

Fans of the American post-punk cabaret singer Amanda Palmer will be familiar with her web presence. As well as the requisite social media hooks (Twitter, MySpace, Facebook and YouTube), Palmer's site offers a variety of purchases. For example, her release *Amanda Palmer Goes Down Under* (2011) can be downloaded as a digital album (in either 320kbps MP3 or FLAC formats) for US$1(or more). A limited-edition CD is also available, as well as numerous bundles which combine the downloaded album with merchandise, including buttons, patches and stickers (for $10), a "phone call from down under bundle" ($500 for a phone or Skype call from Palmer) or a Wine-Time backstage bundle ($1500), which gives the purchaser backstage access to an Amanda Palmer show. At the top of the tree is the "AFP will play at your house" bundle, which for US$5000 bought a private gig for up to fifty guests. And there were other opportunities to engage with Palmer's music. For those with more creative ambitions, there was a remix competition inviting fans to remix the single 'Map Of Tasmania' (2011), with the best remix (judged by a panel that included Palmer) winning $1000.

This wide-ranging approach and philosophy made Amanda Palmer the darling of those who feel there is a new future of music. As the pin-up girl for the new music start-up Bandcamp (having sold $15,000-worth of music and merchandise in the first three minutes of availability), her label-free methods are exemplars of the new music ecology. And her forays into the crowdfunding website Kickstarter resulted in the raising of over $1 million to pay for her next album. Given the Amanda Palmer experience, it is easy to argue that Music 2.0 empowers musicians absolutely. However, the reality is (as usual) more complex. Whilst Palmer no longer has a traditional record label, her music is still available through the new industry intermediaries such as Apple's iTunes, where fans can pay the regular iTunes price for tracks and albums. One of the authors first heard an Amanda Palmer song (as opposed to having heard of her) when it was played on a popular radio station in Sydney. Clearly, there are many ways for musicians to recruit listeners; and there is no single model for "success".

In fact, Amanda Palmer's business model is not so different from the Grateful Dead's from forty years previously. Both dismissed the sale of recorded music as a primary revenue source and focused on areas such as live shows and merchandise. Both built loyal and enthusiastic fan bases – and did so by directly appealing to those fans. Where Palmer had Facebook and Twitter, the Dead created its own mailing list and ticketing office. Whilst the Dead reached out to a small and dedicated cult following of "Deadheads" largely based in and around California, Palmer has a large and loyal fan base across the globe. Clearly the affordances of the new technologies have enabled the likes of Palmer to build relationships with fans in a more effective manner than the Dead ever could – and given her the tools to build not just relationships but viable products that she can sell to her fans. But the motivations and approaches for making and succeeding with music are eerily similar.

The Cathedral and the Bazaar

In *The Cathedral and the Bazaar* (1999) Eric Raymond championed the role of (what he calls) the bazaar in promoting innovation and creativity. Distinguishing the ground-up, chaotic, easily accessible – and ostensibly more democratic – model of a village marketplace from the top-down, hierarchically structured model of the high church, Raymond suggests that greater innovation and value could be created in the more open markets of the former. Using open-source software as his focus, he argues that the traditional software temples (such as Microsoft) are under direct threat from the more open and interactive bazaar approaches exemplified by the Linux operating system. In time, he argued, the open approach would come to dominate – in both innovation and market share. Although this has certainly proven to be the case in particular segments of the software market (for example, the open-source Apache software that serves a large proportion of all websites), it does not appear to be universally true. At the time of writing, Microsoft's Windows operating systems still dominate the personal computer marketplace and its closest competitor is not Linux, but Apple's OSX system, what Raymond would see as another product of the cathedral. Whilst it is arguable that Android is on its way to becoming the dominant operating system in the mobile space, it has only done so with the backing of Google, itself a cathedral in many respects. Of course Linux still exists and has its users, across a wide range of areas,but to suggest that the cathedral model is doomed is hyperbole.

The same comment applies to the broader media space. Even though the accessibility provided by internet technologies has created a global virtual bazaar that allows broad access for both producers and consumers to exchange digital goods, there is a range of models, all of which have provided ways for media producers to engage with their audiences. Traditional cathedrals (often derisively known as the mainstream media) continue to attract large audiences. Curated collections (such as Amazon MP3, Apple's iTunes

Music and App Stores), which might be seen as highly structured and regulated bazaars – along the lines of suburban shopping malls, for example – attract enormous numbers of users whilst also providing reasonable access for media creators (whether native to the bazaar or cathedral) to sell their products. Beyond those edifices, the bazaar remains – the worldwide web enabling all manner of traders to set up stalls displaying their wares. The same is true of music, where, clearly, cathedrals still have a role to play.

The importance of Music 2.0 is not that it will destroy cathedrals, but that it makes bazaars more accessible and allows the creation of a huge range of possibilities in between the two. Access to digital media tools has flattened previously entrenched distinctions and the new media ecology reflects the newly converged media-scape: one in which technologies, industries, social practices and texts converge. We suggest that Music 2.0 might be best understood in the context of such convergences and the new accessibility to distribution channels. In particular, there is a blurring of the various music industries as the distinctions between recording, publishing, performing and retailing begin to disappear. Simultaneously, the range of musical activities from school-hall performance to Wembley Stadium has also been extended. Once invisible acts have now become visible, allowing musicians new opportunities to commercialize their activities. The internet has allowed the industrial processes of music production to be subverted – what used to be conceived of as a singular mass-oriented activity is now more than that. Musicians are realizing that it is possible to make a living by discovering and marketing to (often directly or through new intermediaries) niches that have always existed, but were previously inaccessible. The new opportunities may have subverted but certainly have not replaced the industrial processes that dominated the music industries in recent history. For every Amanda Palmer there is a Lady Gaga. For every Jonathan Coulton, there is a Justin Bieber. In the middle ground between these two extremes there are those artists eking out a living using the new digital technologies.

The reality is that older approaches will co-exist with newer ones. The major labels still exert significant influence in making and breaking a record, but the palpable excitement detectable amongst many musicians arises because older industrial approaches no longer have a monopoly: a record deal is no longer the only way to get an audience for your music.

The Prehistory of Music 2.0

In music, the creation of cathedrals is a relatively recent phenomenon. It was not until the early twentieth century that recording and duplication technologies were sufficiently developed to allow the sale of recorded music to become a viable industry. The initial cost of developing and implementing that technology – and the ongoing expense of production and distribution – required an investment that made it the domain of large enterprises. The affordances of recorded music were such that any industry built around music required economies of scale that were predisposed to a cathedral model.

With each iteration of technology, the structural requirements of the industry remained the same – the advent of mass media via broadcast mechanisms and global distribution tended towards a top-down distribution model where musicians were selected by record companies and granted access to their channels.

The introduction of the internet and increasingly affordable production technologies enabled a challenge to that distribution dominance. Whilst the market power of existing record companies remained, others threatened their monopoly over distributing recorded music. Software companies such as Apple, Microsoft and Google became new intermediaries joining the plethora of independent artists who were themselves suddenly able to access audiences directly – albeit without the marketing clout of large corporations.

And without that marketing clout, innovation returned. Subverting fifty years of practice which had seen a narrowly focused music industry promote a limited range of engagements with musicians (recorded artefacts, highly structured live shows and a limited range of licensed merchandise), the new technologies suddenly empowered artists to conceive of new ways to engage with their audiences, building direct relationships with fans that just were not possible in the record-industry era. Many have called this Music 2.0 but in reality it is little more than the current phase of a continuing and developing relationship that we have with music.

As with all popular media forms, that relationship with music is a social construction. A reading of any cultural history of music can trace the use of music in communities, building on the prevalent oral cultures of the time. The role of the musician was initially a live one – providing audio colour for communal events, triumphant accompaniment to military processions or intimate entertainment to private groups. Economically, much of this performance-based musicianship was predicated on a system of patronage, whereby selected musicians were granted a stipend by a rich benefactor in exchange for their provision of musical services. However, those who were unable to benefit from the system of patronage constructed their own frameworks for generating income, demonstrating an entrepreneurship not normally associated with art. In an earlier chapter we described how classical musicians built audiences and earned their keep in the salons of Paris. That model obviously predates the recorded-music industry and illustrates an alternative construction of music, which saw musicians able to make an "agreeable" living from playing live music in a decidedly non-industrial setting.

Arguably the internet has enabled contemporary musicians to revisit that mode of engagement. For some, what the traditional industry terms piracy is actually publicity – used to build audiences for live shows. Ed Sheeran (who in September 2012 held the distinction of having the most "bittorrented" song in the UK) exemplifies the attitude:

> I sell a lot of tickets. I've sold 1.2 million albums and there's eight million downloads as well, illegally … So nine million people have my record in England, which is quite a nice feeling. You get people who actually want to listen to your songs and come to an event like this in London, who wouldn't necessarily buy the album … You can live off your sales and you can allow people to illegally download it and come to your gigs. My gig tickets are £18 and my album is £8, so it's all relative. (Proffitt 2012)

(Not) the Death of Recorded Music

Of course, the value of recorded music remains the most contentious element of current debates, and whilst it is only a part of the broader digital music ecology, it is still an appropriate point to conclude this book. As we discussed in Chapter 3, recording not only shifted the relationship of music with time and space, but also introduced new techniques of musicianship – for example, the layering of tracks enabled musicians to create something that was impossible to produce in the live environment. The 1970s saw the rise of so-called studio bands, like Steely Dan, who seldom played together live, yet created a large body of recorded work. Not only are such recording techniques now commonplace, but there is much wider access to the tools that afford such creativity. Even as multitrack recording equipment became more widespread, few would have predicted the availability and affordability of tools such as Apple's Garageband application for its iPad. In that context, the social construction of music is unlikely to return to one which is solely based on live performance. But it is likely that the use of the recorded artefact will undergo a further transformation; its availability for wider audience engagement (for example, via Garageband remix as offered by Nine Inch Nails) gestures towards the types of possibilities that continue to be explored.

We need to understand Music 2.0 as part of a bigger historical and social context, one in which technology has always been implicated in changes to production and distribution processes, and where the twentieth-century model is seen as no more than a period of stability in a dynamically evolving realm. It is common for participants in debates over the state of the music industry to emphasize particular losses or gains. So, incumbent major labels will attribute falling sales to piracy, in an attempt to gain political support for legislative action to shore up existing business models. Similarly, those (such as independent musicians) with more to gain from innovative approaches embrace the current changes and argue for political support for their own perspectives. The reality is more nuanced and simply reflects the fact that such tensions are an expected component of the continually contested realm that is the music industry.

This book contextualizes Music 2.0 in that broader understanding of music – with particular emphasis on the notion that the commercialization of music has always been a dynamic, evolving system. The twentieth-century industrialization can be seen as a moment of stability that arose as a consequence of the specific technical and social affordances of the time – and contemporary changes are simply the inevitable result of musicians exploring the possibilities of the new.

To reiterate, though, cultural change happens slowly and is contested, not least by institutions whose very existence depends on the status quo. Despite our assertion that commodifying recorded music as a way of profiting from music could be understood as a mere aberration in the long history of music, it remains the current cultural habit of most of the world's population and is not going to go away anytime soon. Indeed, we are witnessing *displacement* rather than *replacement* as the dominance of the twentieth-century music business is slowly eroded by artists and audiences taking advantage of the new possibilities. Even as institutions reinvent themselves – and are eventually displaced by more responsive ones – our relationship with music will expand inclusively rather than exclusively. It is unlikely that our need for commonality will diminish; just as popular television shows and movies continue to provide much of our shared cultural capital, so too does popular music. Although the dimensions of its impact will no doubt shift (with perhaps more, perhaps fewer, international superstars) – and the mechanisms by which global hits are made are also changing as musicians are discovered via YouTube (viz Justin Bieber) as well as the local pub – the industry's ability to create and market the next musical phenomenon is driven by that peculiar audience hunger to connect via common cultural experience, something that will remain undiminished.

Yet many musicians have sought success by bypassing those industrial processes for recording and distributing music. So-called independents retain control over their artistic output – sometimes forgoing the benefits of a relationship with bigger record companies in order to maintain their artistic integrity. The twentieth-century route to recording success was largely at the whim of those major record companies. The payola scandals (and their successors) exemplified the extent of the industry's control over not only distribution but also exposure to new music. Even if independent bands were successful on smaller labels, it often required the backing of a major to achieve more significant sales.

In Music 2.0, not only are there new intermediaries, but for some artists there is no need for them. Indeed, some have argued that the new technologies have made it possible for truly independent music to thrive – and for business models that were previously marginal to be financially viable. It is undeniable that the possibilities for musicians have been expanded dramatically with the reinvigoration of possibilities that were impossible in a world dominated by a particular model of commodification. For audiences, there are now more ways to discover music than ever before. There is a greater range of music available, more ways to engage with both music and musicians and a depth of relationship with music that has never before been possible. And for musicians, the same expansion of affordances holds true in the other direction – it has never been easier for someone with musical talent to display it to the world. We argue that the industrial model of production, built on global superstars, is unlikely to disappear (guaranteed perhaps by our insatiable appetite for celebrity gossip). But if the broadening of the recorded music marketplace that Music 2.0 allows does displace some of the older models (perhaps seen as a diminishing in the number of those global superstars created by the major record companies), then, for many, that will be a small price to pay – and one worth paying.

Appendix

Sections of this book are based on original research undertaken by the authors during the course of 2007. The research consisted of 42 in-depth interviews (face-to-face and telephone) with Australian musicians, supplemented by an on-line survey with over 200 participants. The on-line survey responses provided a good overview of musician attitudes towards the internet, but richer material was gleaned from the interviews – which unpacked (and confirmed) the survey responses and explored territory more directly relevant to this book.

The interviews (undertaken between April and November 2007) consisted of open-ended questions and were conducted with a wide range of musicians canvassed via contacts (both personal and professional) and unsolicited email. The respondents included successful popular artists with top 10 hits, classical music professionals and musicians on the local gig circuit with day jobs. Most responded on the condition of anonymity. Although not a complete breakdown of respondents, the following table provides a picture of the scope of the interviews.

Musician category (at interview)	Number of interviewees
Musicians with chart success (at least 1 Australian or international top 40 "hit")	19
Other professional musicians (self-defined, including classical)	15
Aspiring musicians/non-professional (mostly young bands with local gigs)	8

Those interviewed were initially asked about their attitudes towards the internet in terms of their musical practice, and during the course of the conversations their views on the evolving nature of professional music emerged. Whilst it would be inappropriate to draw singular conclusions from such a diverse group of musicians, there was striking similarity in many of the opinions expressed, which are reflected in this book.

Bibliography

Albanesius, Chloe (2011). "Apple Unveils Updated iPod Nano, Touch". *PC Mag.* http://www.pcmag.com/article2/0,2817,2394061,00.asp (accessed 17 November 2011).

Albini, Steve (1994). "The Problem with Music". *Maximum Rock n' Roll* 133 (June 1994). Archived at http://www.negativland.com/news/?page_id=17 (accessed 11 January 2012).

Alderman, John (2001). *Sonic Boom: Napster, Mp3, and the New Pioneers of Music.* Cambridge, MA: Perseus Books.

Anderson, Chris (2006). "The Rise and Fall of the Hit". *Wired.com.* http://www.wired.com/wired/archive/14.07/longtail.html (accessed 6 January 2012).

Anderson, Nate (2010). "Judge Slashes 'Monstrous' P2P Award by 97% to $54,000". *Ars Technica.* http://arstechnica.com/tech-policy/news/2010/01/judge-slashes-monstrous-jammie-thomas-p2p-award-by-35x.ars (accessed 14 February 2012).

Anonymous (2011). "If Only Joel Lived in China". *Joel Fights Back,* 28 April. http://joelfightsback.com/#/2011/05/if-only-joel-lived-in-china/ (accessed 25 March 2012).

Apple (2011). "iTunes Music Aggregators". *Apple.* Archived at http://web.archive.org/web/20110725125649/https://itunesconnect.apple.com/webObjects/iTunesConnect.woa/wa/displayAggregators?ccTypeId=3 (accessed 21 July 2012).

Aufderheide, Pat, and Peter Jaszi (2008). "Recut, Reframe, Recycle: Quoting Copyrighted Material in User-generated Video". *Center for Social Media.* http://www.centerforsocialmedia.org/fair-use/best-practices/online-video/recut-reframe-recycle (accessed 18 November 2011).

Bangeman, Eric (2007). "Sony BMG's Chief Anti-Piracy Lawyer: 'Copying' Music You Own Is Stealing". *Ars Technica.* http://arstechnica.com/tech-policy/2007/10/sony-bmgs-chief-anti-piracy-lawyer-copying-music-you-own-is-stealing/ (accessed 12 October 2011).

Barton, Laura (2005). "The Question: Have the Arctic Monkeys Changed the Music Business?" *Guardian,* 25 October. http://www.guardian.co.uk/music/2005/oct/25/popandrock.arcticmonkeys (accessed 14 July 2011).

BBC (May 2006). "The Online Music Revolution". *The Money Programme.*

BBC News (2007a). "Fans Crash Radiohead Site". http://news.bbc.co.uk/2/hi/entertainment/7024130.stm (accessed 19 July 2011).

BBC News (2007b). "Madonna Signs Radical Record Deal". http://news.bbc.co.uk/2/hi/entertainment/7047969.stm (accessed 23 July 2011).

Bemis, Alec (2005). "Busking for Stardom". *LA Weekly.* http://www.laweekly.com/2005-12-01/calendar/busking-for-stardom/ (accessed 19 April 2011).

Benedikt, Michael (1991). "Cyberspace: Some Proposals", in Michael Benedikt (ed.), *Cyberspace: First Steps.* Cambridge, MA: MIT Press, pp. 119–224.

Benjamin, Walter (1992). "The Work of Art in the Age of Mechanical Reproduction", in *Illuminations*. London: Fontana Press, pp. 211–44. (First published in English in 1968.)

Billboard (1999). 12 June, p. 75.

Billboard (2000). 8 July, p. 19.

Blumberg, Alex (2011). "Is This Man a Snuggie?" *NPR Planet Money*, 20 May. http://www.npr.org/blogs/money/2011/05/20/136496085/the-friday-podcast-is-this-man-a-snuggie (accessed 24 May 2011).

Boehlert, Eric (2000). "Four Little Words". *Salon.com*, 28 August. http://dir.salon.com/ent/music/feature/2000/08/28/work_for_hire/index.htm (accessed 12 November 2011).

Boehlert, Eric (2001). "Pay for Play". *Salon.com*, 15 March. http://www.salon.com/2001/03/14/payola_2/ (accessed 29 September 2011).

Boehlert, Eric (2002). "Will Congress Tackle Pay-for-Play". *Salon.com*, 26 June. http://www.salon.com/2002/06/25/pfp-congress/ (accessed 29 September 2011).

Bohlman, Philip V. (2001). "Ontologies of Music", in Nicholas Cook and Mark Everist (eds), *Rethinking Music*. Oxford, New York: Oxford University Press, pp. 17–34.

Bolger, Timothy (2000). "Justin Bieber Mall 'Riot' Case Conference Postponed". *Long Island Press*. http://www.longislandpress.com/2010/10/13/justin-bieber-mall-riot-case-conference-postponed/ (accessed 17 April 2011).

Bourdieu, Pierre (1984). *Distinction: A Social Critique of the Judgment of Taste*. London: Routledge.

Brereton, Ian (2009). "The Beginning of a New Age? The Unconscionability of the '360-Degree' Deal". *Cardozo Arts and Entertainment Law Journal* 27.1 (2009): 167–97.

Brindley, Paul (2000). *New Musical Entrepreneurs*. London: Institute for Public Policy Research.

British Phonographic Industry (BPI) (2012). "Music Sales Slip in 2011 But Digital Singles and Albums Grow Strongly". http://www.bpi.co.uk/assets/files/music%20sales%20slip%20in%202011%20but%20digital%20grow%20strongly.pdf (accessed 23 January 2012).

Browne, David (2011). "Record Biz Braces for Legal Battles over Copyright Law". *Rolling Stone*. http://www.rollingstone.com/music/news/record-biz-braces-for-legal-battles-over-copyright-law-20110902 (accessed 3 March 2012).

Bruns, Axel (2005). *Gatewatching: Collaborative Online News Production*. New York: Peter Lang.

Bruns, Axel (2008). *Blogs, Wikipedia, Second Life, and Beyond: From Production to Produsage*. New York: Peter Lang.

Bruns, Axel (2011). "News Produsage in a Pro-Am Mediasphere: Why Citizen Journalism Matters", in Graham Meikle and Guy Redden (eds), *News Online*. Basingstoke: Palgrave Macmillan, pp. 132–47.

Buckley, David, and John Shepherd (2003). "Stardom", in John Shepherd, David Horn, Dave Laing, Paul Oliver and Peter Wicke (eds), *Continuum Encyclopedia of Popular Music of the World*. London, New York: Continuum, pp. 366–9.

Burry, Kenneth, and Jay Cooper (2001). "The Work Made for Hire Conundrum". Presented at conference on *Talent in the New Millennium: The International Association of Entertainment Lawyers*, MIDEM 2001, Cannes.

Busch, Richard (2012). "Major Labels as Dinosaurs". *Forbes*. http://www.forbes.com/sites/richardbusch/2012/03/27/major-record-labels-as-dinosaurs/ (accessed 23 April 2012).

Buxton, David (1990). "Rock Music, the Star System and the Rise of Consumerism", in Simon Frith and Andrew Goodwin (eds), *Rock, Pop and the Written Word*. London: Routledge, pp. 366–77.

Byrne, David, and Thom Yorke (2007). "David Byrne and Thom Yorke on the Real Value of Music". *Wired.com*. http://www.wired.com/entertainment/music/magazine/16-01/ff_yorke?currentPage=all (accessed 4 January 2012).

Callon, Michel, and Bruno Latour (1981). "Unscrewing the Big Leviathan: How Actors Macro-Structure Reality and How Sociologists Help Them to Do So", in Karin Knorr-Cetina and Aron V. Cicourel (eds), *Advances in Social Theory and Methodology: Towards an Integration of Micro and Macro-Sociology*. Boston, London: Routledge, pp. 277–303.

Caplan, Brian D. (2012). "Navigating US Copyright Termination Rights". *WIPO.int*. http://www.wipo.int/wipo_magazine/en/2012/04/article_0005.html (accessed 9 September 2012).

Carroll, Michael (2006). "Creative Commons and the New Intermediaries". *Michigan State Law Review* (Spring): 45–66.

Chanan, Michael (1995). *Repeated Takes: A Short History of Recording and Its Effects on Music*. London, New York: Verso.

Chandrasekaran, Rajiv, and Elizabeth Corcoran (1997). "Smut Ruling Ratifies the Internet's Founding Principles". *Washington Post*, 27 June. http://www.washingtonpost.com/wp-srv/tech/analysis/decency/founding.htm (accessed 17 September 2011).

Christensen, Clayton (1997). *The Innovator's Dilemma: When New Technologies Cause Great Firms to Fail*. Boston: Harvard Business School Press.

CmdrTaco (2001). *Slashdot*. http://slashdot.org/story/01/10/23/1816257/apple-releases-ipod (accessed 21 September 2011).

Coulton, Jonathan (2011). "On Snuggies and Business Models". *Jonathan Coulton*, 23 May. http://www.jonathancoulton.com/2011/05/23/on-snuggies-and-business-models/ (accessed 26 May 2011).

Coyle, Jake (2009). "Kutcher all of a Twitter after reaching magic million". *Sydney Morning Herald*. http://www.smh.com.au/news/entertainment/kutcher-all-of-a-twitter-after-reaching-magic-million/2009/04/18/1240008826939.html (accessed 30 June 2011).

Cross, Mary (2011). *Bloggerati, Twitterati: How Blogs and Twitter Are Transforming Popular Culture*. Oxford: Praeger.

Daniel, Eric, C. Denis Mee and Mark H. Clark (1999). *Magnetic Recording: The First 100 Years*. New York: IEEE Press.

Dannen, Frederic (1990). *Hit Men: Power Brokers and Fast Money Inside the Music Business*. New York: First Vintage Books Edition.

David, Matthew (2010). *Peer to Peer and the Music Industry: The Criminalisation of Sharing*. London: Sage.

de Certeau, Michel (1984). *The Practice of Everyday Life*. Berkeley; Los Angeles; London: University of California Press.

DeNora, Tia (2000). *Music in Everyday Life*. Cambridge: Cambridge University Press.

Donaldson v. *Becket* (1774) 17 *Cobbett, Parliamentary History*, col. 953.

Draper, Paul (2007). "Music Two-Point-Zero: How Participatory Culture Is Reclaiming Knowledge, Power and Value Systems from the Inside Out". Queensland Conservatorium Research Centre Twilight Series Public Lecture, 9 October 2007. http://www29.griffith.edu.au/radioimersd/images/stories/draper_091007_twilight_lecture.pdf (accessed 14 September 2011).

du Lac, J. Freedom (2006). "Giving Indie Acts a Plug, or Pulling It". *Washington Post*. http://www.washingtonpost.com/wp-dyn/content/article/2006/04/28/AR2006042800457.html (accessed 23 August 2011).

Dubber, Andrew (2007). *New Music Strategies: The 20 Things You Must Know about Online Music*. New Music Strategies. http://newmusicstrategies.com/wp-content/uploads/2008/06/nms.pdf (accessed 23 January 2012).

Economist, The (2008). "From Major to Minor". http://www.economist.com/node/10498664 (accessed 26 October 2011).

EFF (2008). "RIAA v. The People: Five Years Later". *Electronic Frontier Foundation*. https://www.eff.org/wp/riaa-v-people-five-years-later (accessed 23 February 2012).

Eisenberg, Evan (1987). *The Recording Angel: Music, Records and Culture from Aristotle to Zappa*. New York: McGraw-Hill Book Company.

Elberse, Anita (2008). "Should You Invest in the Long Tail?" *Harvard Business Review* 86.7 (July): 88–96.

Elder, Sean (2002). "The Death of Rolling Stone". *Salon.com*. http://www.salon.com/2002/06/28/rollingstone/ (accessed 29 April 2011).

Fagin, Matthew, Frank Pasquale and Kim Weatherall (2002). "Beyond Napster: Using Antitrust Law to Advance and Enhance Online Music Distribution". *Boston University Journal of Science and Technology Law* 8 (Summer): 451–573.

Fairchild, Charles (2005). "The Currency of Collusion: The Circulation of Embrace of the Ethic of Authenticity in Mediated Musical Communities". *Journal of Popular Music* 17.3 (December): 301–23.

Feather, John (1988). "Where Did Copyright Come From?" *European Intellectual Property Review* 12: 377–80.

Feather, John (1994). *Publishing, Piracy and Politics: An Historical Study of Copyright in Britain*. London: Mansell.

Finnegan, Ruth (2007). *The Hidden Musicians: Music-making in an English Town*. 2nd edn. Middletown, CT: Wesleyan University Press.

Flew, Terry (2009). *New Media: An Introduction*. Melbourne: Oxford University Press.

Fraunhofer Institute for Integrated Circuits (n.d.). "The Story of Mp3". *Fraunhofer Institute for Integrated Circuits*. http://www.mp3-history.com/en/the_story_of_mp3.html (accessed 2 March 2013).

Freund, Jesse (1999). "Listen Up". *Wired.com*. http://www.wired.com/wired/archive/7.03/chuckd_pr.html (accessed 9 April 2012).

Frith, Simon (1988). "The Industrialization of Music", in Simon Frith (ed.), *Music for Pleasure*. New York: Routledge, pp. 11–23.

Frith, Simon (2006). "The Industrialization of Music", in Andy Bennett, Barry Shank and Jason Toynbee (eds), *The Popular Music Studies Reader*. Oxford, New York: Routledge, pp. 231–38.

Frith, Simon (2007). *Taking Popular Music Seriously: Selected Essays*. Farnham, Surrey: Ashgate.

Gibson, William (1989). "Rocket Radio". *Rolling Stone*, 15 June, 85–7.

Gillmor, Dan (2006). *We the Media: Grassroots Journalism by the People for the People*. Sebastopol, CA: O'Reilly Media.

Godin, Seth (2010). *Linchpin: Are You Indispensable?* New York: Penguin.

Gordon, Steve (2005). *The Future of the Music Business: How to Succeed with the New Digital Technologies*. San Francisco: Backbeat Books.

Graff, Gary (2012). "Def Leppard Recording 'Forgeries' of Old Hits to Spite Label". *Billboard. com*. http://www.billboard.com/#/news/def-leppard-recording-forgeries-of-old-hits-1007484752.story (accessed 5 July 2012).

Gronow, Pekka, and Ilpo Saunio (1998). *An International History of the Recording Industry*. London, New York: Cassell.

Guardian, The (2009). "Inside Ashton Kutcher's World of Twitter". *The Guardian Lost In Showbiz Blog*, 21 April. http://www.guardian.co.uk/lifeandstyle/2009/apr/21/ashton-kutcher-celebrity-twitter (accessed 29 January 2012).

Guardian, The (2012). "Leonard Cohen – Old Ideas: Exclusive Album Stream". *Guardian Music Blog*, 23 January. http://www.guardian.co.uk/music/musicblog/2012/jan/23/leonard-cohen-old-ideas-stream?newsfeed=true (accessed 24 January 2012).

Hall, Phillip W., Jr (2002). "Smells Like Slavery: Unconscionability in Recording Industry Contracts". *Hastings Communications and Entertainment Law Journal* 25.1 (2002):189–229.

Hargittai, Eszter (2000). "Radio's Lessons for the Internet". *Communications of the ACM* 43.1: 51–7.

Hartley, John (2000). "Communicative Democracy in a Redactional Society: The Future of Journalism Studies". *Journalism: Theory, Practice and Criticism* 1.1: 39–48.

Harvey, Eric (2011). "Same as the Old Boss? Changes, Continuities, and Careers in the Digital Music Era", in Mark Deuze (ed.), *Managing Media Work*. London: Sage, pp. 237–48.

Hervey, Scott (2002). "Future of Online Music: Labels and Artists". *Transnational Lawyer* 15.n (Spring 2002): 279–92.

Hesmondhalgh, David (2006). "The British Dance Music Industry: A Case Study of Independent Cultural Production", in Andy Bennett, Barry Shank and Jason Toynbee (eds), *The Popular Music Studies Reader*. London: Routledge, pp. 246–52.

Heyman, Barry (2012). "Termination Rights in Sound Recordings". *Heylaw*. http://heylaw.com/resources/articles/termination-rights-and-sound-recordings/ (accessed 11 August 2012).

Hoffman, Jan (2009). "Justin Bieber Is Living the Dream". *New York Times*. http://www.nytimes.com/2010/01/03/fashion/03bieber.html (accessed 4 March 2012).

Holmes, David (2005). *Communication Theory: Media, Technology and Society*. London: Sage.

Ian, Janis (2002). "The Internet Debacle – an Alternative View". *Performing Songwriter* 61 (May 2002). http://www.janisian.com/reading/internet.php (accessed 19 November 2011).

IFPI (2012). "Digital Music Report 2012: Expanding Choice, Going Global". *International Federation of the Phonographic Industry*. http://www.ifpi.org/content/library/DMR 2012.pdf (accessed 13 January 2012).

Ingham, Tim (2012). "Revealed: The True Value of '360' Deals to Labels". *Music Week* http://www.musicweek.com/news/read/360-deals-spark-76m-income-for-labels-in-2011/052043 (accessed 20 November 2012).

James, Robin (1990). *Cassette Mythos*. Brooklyn, NY: Autonomedia.

Jenkins, Henry (2006). *Convergence Culture: Where Old and New Media Collide*. New York: New York University Press.

Kakutani, Michiko (2010). "Company on the Verge of a Social Breakthrough". *New York Times*, 7 June. http://www.nytimes.com/2010/06/08/books/08book.html (accessed 21 July 2011).

Karaganis, Joe (2011). "Copyright Infringement and Enforcement in the US". *American Assembly*. http://piracy.americanassembly.org/get-the-copy-culture-report/ (accessed 19 January 2012).

Katz, Jon (1997). "Birth of a Digital Nation". *Wired*. http://www.wired.com/wired/archive/5.04/netizen.html (accessed 12 March 2012).

Katz, Mark (2010). *Capturing Sound: How Technology Has Changed Music*. Berkeley and Los Angeles: University of California Press.

Keen, Andrew (2007). *The Cult of the Amateur: How Today's Internet Is Killing Our Culture*. New York: Doubleday/Currency.

Kelly, Kevin (2005). "We Are the Web". *Wired*. http://www.wired.com/wired/archive/13.08/tech.html (accessed 4 February 2012).

Kelly, Kevin (2007). "Technology Wants to Be Free". *The Technium*, 14 November. http://www.kk.org/thetechnium/archives/2007/11/technology_want.php (accessed 24 November 2011).

Kelly, Kevin (2008a). "Better Than Free". *The Technium*, 3 January. http://www.kk.org/thetechnium/archives/2008/01/better_than_fre.php. (accessed 24 November 2011).

Kelly, Kevin (2008b). "1,000 True Fans". *The Technium*, 4 March. http://www.kk.org/thetechnium/archives/2008/03/1000_true_fans.php (accessed 24 November 2011).

Kelly, Mark (2008). "The Internet Is a Double-edged Sword for Music". *The Telegraph*, 7 August. http://blogs.telegraph.co.uk/technology/shanerichmond/4842187/The_internet_is_a_doubleedged_sword_for_music/ (accessed 18 March 2012).

Kenner, Rob (1999). "My Hollywood!" *Wired*. http://www.wired.com/wired/archive/7.10/microcinema.html (accessed 7 July 2012).

Keyes, J. Michael (2004). "Musical Musings: The Case for Rethinking Music Copyright Protection". *Michigan Telecommunications and Technology Law Review* 10.2 (Winter 2004): 407–33.

Khare, Rohit, and D. C. Denison (1996). "Interview: Tim Berners Lee on Simplicity, Standards and 'Intercreativity'." *WWW Journal*. 1.3 (1996). http://web.archive.org/web/19980114070555/w3journal.com/3/s1.interview.html (accessed 28 February 2011).

Kirkpatrick, David (2010). *The Facebook Effect: The Inside Story of the Company That Is Connecting the World*. New York: Simon & Schuster.

Knopper, Steve (2009). *Appetite for Self-Destruction*. New York: Free Press.

Kozinski, Alex (1993). "Trademarks Unplugged". *New York University Law Review* 68.4 (October): 960–78.

Kracauer, Siegfried (1972). *Orpheus in Paris: Offenbach and the Paris of His Time*. New York: Vienna House. Cited in Michael Chanan (1999), *From Handel to Hendrix*. London: Verso, p. 35.

Kusek, David, and Gerd Leonhard (2005). *The Future of Music: Manifesto for the Digital Music Revolution*. Boston: Berklee Press.

Laing, Dave (2003). "Copyright" , in John Shepherd, David Horn, Dave Laing, Paul Oliver and Peter Wicke (eds), *Continuum Encyclopedia of Popular Music of the World*. London: Continuum, pp. 480–93.

Laningham, Scott (2006). "DeveloperWorks Interviews: Tim Berners-Lee". *Ibm.com*. http://www.ibm.com/developerworks/podcast/dwi/cm-int082206txt.html (accessed 3 August 2012).

Laughey, Dan (2007). "Music Media in Young People's Everyday Lives", in Jamie Sexton (ed.), *Music, Sound and Multimedia: From the Live to the Virtual*. Edinburgh: Edinburgh University Press, pp. 172–87.

Lauria, Peter (2008). "A 'Signature' Deal". *New York Post*. http://www.nypost.com/seven/10192007/business/a_signature_deal.htm (accessed 20 March 2011).

Lear, Courtney (n.d.). "U.K.'s Enter Shikari Scores Without Label". *Billboard.com*. http://www.billboard.com/articles/news/1053180/uks-enter-shikari-scores-without-label (accessed 19 December 2011).

Leonhard, Gerd (2008). *Music 2.0: Essays on the Future of the Music Business*. http://lulu.com (accessed 2 October 2012).

Lessig, Lawrence (2008). *Remix: Making Art and Commerce Thrive in the Hybrid Economy*. London: Bloomsbury Academic.

Levinson, Paul (1997). *The Soft Edge: A Natural History and Future of the Information Revolution*. London: Routledge.

Levy, Steven (1995). *Hackers: Heroes of the Computer Revolution*. New York: Delta.

Levy, Steven (2006). *The Perfect Thing: How the iPod Shuffles Commerce, Culture and Coolness*. New York: Simon & Schuster.

Love, Courtney (2001). "Love's Manifesto". *Indie Music*. http://www.indie-music.com/modules.php?name=News&file=article&sid=820 (accessed 23 October 2011).

McHugh, Kenna (2011). "Justin Bieber Movie Premiere Hits Social Media – Live Premiere on Facebook, Twitter & Livestream". *Social Times*. http://socialtimes.com/justin-bieber-never-say-never-live premiere-on-facebook-Twitter-livestream_b37810 (accessed 12 February 2011).

McLuhan, Marshall (1964) *Understanding Media: The Extensions of Man*. London: Routledge & Kegan Paul.

McManus, Sean (2010). "How to Get Your Music into iTunes and Amazon MP3". *www.sean.co.uk*. http://www.sean.co.uk/a/musicjournalism/var/how_to_sell_your_music_on_itunes_amazon_mp3.shtm (accessed 30 November 2011)

Mann, Charles (2000). "The Heavenly Jukebox". *Atlantic Online*. http://www.theatlantic.com/past/docs/issues/2000/09/mann.htm (accessed 12 October 2011).

Manuel, Peter (1993). *Cassette Culture*. Chicago: University of Chicago Press.

Marshall, Lee (2005). *Bootlegging: Romanticism and Copyright in the Music Industry*. London: Sage.

Marshall, P. David (1997). *Celebrity and Power: Fame and Contemporary Culture*. Minneapolis: University of Minnesota Press.

Martland, Peter (1997). *Since Records Began: EMI, the First 100 Years*. London: Batsford.

Masnick, Mike (2010). "The Future of Music Business Models (and Those Who Are Already

There)". *Techdirt*. http://www.techdirt.com/articles/20091119/1634117011/future-music-business-models-those-who-are-already-there.shtml (accessed 25 April 2011).

Maul, Anthony (2004). "Are the Major Labels Sandbagging Online Music? An Antitrust Analysis of Strategic Licensing Practices". *Journal of Legislation and Public Policy* 7.1 (Fall 2003): 365–92.

Meikle, Graham, and Sherman Young (2012). *Media Convergence: Networked Digital Media in Everyday Life*. Basingstoke: Palgrave Macmillan.

Mellencamp, John (2009). "On My Mind: The State of the Music Business". *Huffington Post*. http://www.huffingtonpost.com/john-mellencamp/on-my-mind-the-state-of-t_b_177836.html (accessed 15 November 2011).

Millard, Andre (2005). *America on Record: A History of Recorded Sound*. New York: Cambridge University Press.

Mnookin, Seth (2007). "Universal's CEO Once Called iPod Users Thieves. Now He's Giving Songs Away". *Wired.com*, 27 November. http://www.wired.com/entertainment/music/magazine/15-12/mf_morris?currentPage=all (accessed 24 March 2011).

Moore, Gordon E. (1965). "Cramming More Components onto Integrated Circuits". *Electronics* 38.8 (1965): 4–7.

MTV (2012). "Smell of Success: Bieber Perfume Sells Every Minute". *MTV UK*. http://www.mtv.co.uk/news/justin-bieber/361526-bieber-perfume-girlfriend (accessed 13 August 2012).

Mulligan, Mark (2011). "Why the Access Versus Ownership Debate Isn't Going to Resolve Itself Anytime Soon". *Music Industry Blog*, 9 December. http://musicindustryblog.wordpress.com/2011/12/09/why-the-access-versus-ownership-debate-isnt-going-to-resolve-itself-anytime-soon/ (accessed 21 December 2011).

Murfett, Andrew (2007). "Instant CDs Put Brass in Musicians' Pockets". *The Age*. http://www.theage.com.au/news/business/instant-live-cds-put-brass-in-musicians-pockets/2007/07/08/1183833344192.html (accessed 20 January 2012).

Music United (2001). "Anti-Piracy Commercial". http://www.youtube.com/watch?v=CORBDvuBz9o (accessed 20 January 2012).

Nathan, John (1999). *Sony*. Boston: Houghton Mifflin Company.

Naughton, John (1999). *A Brief History of the Future: The Origins of the Internet*. London: Phoenix.

Negroponte, Nicholas (1996). *Being Digital*. New York: Vintage Books.

Nelson, Starr (2001). "Rock and Roll Royalties, Copyrights and Contracts of Adhesion: Why Musicians May Be Chasing Waterfalls". *John Marshall Review of Intellectual Property Law* 1.1 (Fall 2001): 163–78.

Norman, Donald (1999). *The Invisible Computer: Why Good Products Can Fail*. Cambridge, MA: MIT Press.

OECD [Organization for Economic Co-operation and Development] (2007). "Participative Web and User-created Content: Web 2.0, Wikis and Social Networking". *OECD*. http://www.oecd.org/document/40/0,3343,en_2649_34223_39428648_1_1_1_1,00.html (accessed 17 October 2012).

O'Reilly, Tim (2005). "What Is Web 2.0? Design Patterns and Business Models for the Next Generation of Software". *O'Reilly Media*. http://oreilly.com/web2/archive/what-is-web-20.html (accessed 16 October 2012).

O'Sullivan, Tim, John Hartley, Danny Saunders, Martin Montgomery and John Fiske (1994). *Key Concepts in Communications*, 2nd edn. London: Routledge.

Ong, Walter (1982). *Orality and Literacy: The Technologizing of the Word*. London: Methuen.

Pareles, Jon (2002). "David Bowie, 21st Century Entrepreneur". *New York Times*. http://www.nytimes.com/2002/06/09/arts/david-bowie-21st-century-entrepreneur.html (accessed 23 November 2011).

Park, Dave (2005). "Aren't Fooling Around". *Prefix.com*, 21 November. http://www.prefixmag.com/features/arctic-monkeys/arent-fooling-around-part-1-of-2/12565/ (accessed 23 July 2011).

Parlor Songs Academy (n.d.). "America's Publishing History: The Story of Tin Pan Alley". *Parlorsongs.com*. http://www.parlorsongs.com/insearch/tinpanalley/tinpanalley.php (accessed 3 August 2011).

Peddie, Ian (2006). *The Resisting Muse*. Aldershot: Ashgate.

Pelly, Jenn (2012). "Death Grips". *Pitchfork*. http://pitchfork.com/features/interviews/9004-death-gripz/ (accessed 3 January 2013).

Peoples, Glenn (2011). "EMI Signs International Licensing Deal with Beatport". *Billboard. biz.* http://www.billboard.biz/bbbiz/industry/record-labels/emi-signs-international-licensing-deal-with-1005027392.story (accessed 12 December 2011).

Pinch, Trevor, and Wiebe Bijker (1987). "The Social Construction of Facts and Artifacts: Or How the Sociology of Science and the Sociology of Technology Might Benefit Each Other", in Wiebe Bijker, Thomas Hughes and Trevor Pinch (eds), *The Social Construction of Technological Systems: New Directions in the Sociology and History of Technology*. Cambridge, MA: MIT Press, pp. 17–50.

Proffitt, Brian (2012). "BitTorrent Downloads Booming – and Benefitting Musicians". *Read-Writeweb / Biz*. http://www.readwriteweb.com/biz/2012/09/bittorrent-downloads-booming-and-benefitting-musicians.php (accessed 20 September 2012).

Protalinski, Emil (2008). "Watch It Live: Facebook 2011 f8 developer conference." *Zdnet.com*. http://www.zdnet.com/blog/facebook/watch-it-live-facebook-2011-f8-developer-conference/3916 (accessed 24 September 2011).

Raymond, Eric (1999). *The Cathedral and the Bazaar: Musings on Linux and Open Source by an Accidental Revolutionary*. Sebastapol, CA: O'Reilly Media.

Recording Industry Association of America v. Diamond Multimedia Systems 180 F.3d 1072 (9th Cir., 1999).

Reed, Everett (2007). *Ovations and Encores: The Musician's Guide to Getting the Best Response from Your Audience*. Sherman Oaks, CA: Aspen Grove Music.

Resnikoff, Paul (2011). "The Comprehensive Guide to Reclaiming Your Old Masters". *DigitalMusicNews*.http://www.digitalmusicnews.com/stories/082910termination (accessed 12 May 2012).

Reznor, Trent (2007). "My Thoughts on What to Do as a New/Unknown Artist". *Forum.NIN.com*, 19 November. http://forum.nin.com/bb/read.php?30,767183,767183 (accessed 19 October 2011).

Roberts, Michael (2002). "Papa's Got a Brand-new Bag: Big Music's Post-Fordist Regime and the Role of Independent Music Labels", in Norman Kelley (ed.), *Rhythm and Business: The Political Economy of Black Music*. New York: Akashic Books, pp. 24–43.

Rohter, Larry (2011). "Record Industry Braces for Artists' Battles over Song Rights". *New York*

Times, 15 August. http://www.nytimes.com/2011/08/16/arts/music/springsteen-and-others-soon-eligible-to-recover-song-rights.html (accessed 5 September 2011).

Rosen, Jay (2012). "The People Formerly Known as the Audience", in Michael Mandiberg (ed.), *The Social Media Reader*. New York: New York University Press, pp. 13–16.

Rossman, Gabriel (2012). *Climbing the Charts: What Radio Airplay Tells Us about the Diffusion of Innovation*. Princeton: Princeton University Press.

Rowe, Dorothy (2002). "Look at Me". *The Guardian*, 9 September. http://media.guardian.co.uk/realitytv/story/0,7521,788628,00.html (accessed 18 October 2012).

Rushe, Dominic (2011). "Justin Bieber Is More Influential Online Than the Dalai Lama or US President". *The Guardian*, 2 January. http://www.guardian.co.uk/media/2011/jan/02/klout-social-media-networking (accessed 23 March 2012).

Samuelson, Pamela (2007). "Preliminary Thoughts on Copyright Reform". *Utah Law Review* 3: 551–72.

Sandall, Robert (2007). "Off the Record". *Prospect* 137 (August): 28–33.

Segil, Larraine (2001). *Fastalliances: Power Your E-Business*. New York: John Wiley & Sons.

Segaller, Stephen (1998). *Nerds 2.0.1: A Brief History of the Internet*. New York: TV Books.

Shuker, Roy (1998). *Popular Music: The Key Concepts*. New York: Routledge.

Sibley, Jake (2001). "Interview: Peter Spellman". *Musicians' Exchange* archived at http://web.archive.org/web/20050924034622/http://musicians.about.com/library/weekly/aa021501a.htm (accessed 24 July 2011).

Smirke, Richard (2012). "Gotye's Smash Hit Almost Didn't Happen". *Billboard.com*. http://www.billboard.com/#/news/gotye-s-smash-hit-almost-didn-t-happen-1006759152.story (accessed 11 June 2012).

Sparks, Glenn (2010). *Media Effects Research: A Basic Introduction*. Boston: Wadsworth.

Spellman, Peter (2002). *The Musician's Internet: On-line Strategies for Success in the Music Industry*. Boston: Berklee Press.

Sterne, Jonathan (2012). *MP3: The Meaning of a Format*. Durham, NC: Duke University Press.

Stoll, Clifford (1995). "The Internet? Bah!" *TheDailyBeast.com*. http://www.thedailybeast.com/newsweek/1995/02/26/the-internet-bah.html (accessed 23 July 2011).

Street, John (1986). *Rebel Rock*. Oxford: Blackwell.

Sweney, Mark (2012). "NME and Q Suffer Sales Declines to the Tune of 20% Year on Year". *The Guardian*, 16 August. http://www.guardian.co.uk/media/2012/aug/16/nme-q-magazine-sales-declines (accessed 14 July 2011).

Sydell, Laura (2011). "Fractured Industry: Companies That Serve Musicians Without Deals". *NPR Music*. http://www.npr.org/blogs/therecord/2011/01/27/133274068/fractured-industry-companies-that-serve-musicians-without-deals (accessed 14 April 2011).

Topspin (2008). "GRAMMY Northwest MusicTech Summit Keynote". *Topspin*. http://web.archive.org/web/20110717074901/http://www.topspinmedia.com/2008/11/grammy-northwest-musictech-summit-keynote (accessed 24 May 2012).

Torremans, Paul, and Carmen Otero García Castrillón (2012). "Reversionary Copyright: A Ghost of the Past or a Current Trap to Assignments of Copyright?" *Intellectual Property Quarterly* 2: 77–93.

Toynbee, Jason (2006). "Copyright, the Work and Phonographic Orality in Music". *Social and Legal Studies* 15.1 (March 2006): 77–99.

Tynan, Dan (2006). "The 25 Worst Tech Products of All Time". *PC World*. http://web. archive.org/web/20110701050236/http://www.pcworld.com/article/125772-3/ the_25_worst_tech_products_of_all_time.html (accessed 26 June 2012).

Tyrangiel, Josh (2007). "Radiohead Says: Pay What You Want". *Time Entertainment*. http:// www.time.com/time/arts/article/0,8599,1666973,00.html (accessed 21 October 2011).

US Congress. House. Committee on the Judiciary (2000a). "United States Copyright Office and Works Made for Hire". Subcommittee on Courts and Intellectual Property of the Committee on the Judiciary, 25 May. http://commdocs.house.gov/committees/ judiciary/hju65223.000/hju65223_0f.htm (accessed 20 June 2012).

US Congress. House. Committee on the Judiciary (2000b). 15 June. http://judiciary.house. gov/legacy/frit0615.htm (accessed 19 June 2012).

Van Bogart, John W. C. (1995). *Magnetic Tape Storage and Handling: A Guide for Libraries and Archives*. Washington, DC: The Commission on Preservation and Access.

Van Buskirk, Eliot (2010). "April 9, 1860: Phonoautogram Records Sound, But Doesn't Reproduce It". *Wired.com*, 9 April. http://www.wired.com/thisdayintech/2010/04/ 0409scott-phonoautogram (accessed 20 March 2011).

Visible Measures (2012). "Update: Kony Social Video Campaign Tops 100 Million Views". *Visible Measures*, 12 March. http://corp.visiblemeasures.com/news-and-events/ blog/bid/79626/Update-Kony-Social-Video-Campaign-Tops-100-Million-Views (accessed 14 March 2012).

Walthal et al. v. *Corey Rusk et al.* 172 F3d 481 (7th Cir., 1999).

Wardrip-Fruin, Noah (2003). "The Technology and Society", in Noah Wardrip-Fruin and Nick Montford (eds), *The New Media Reader*. Cambridge, MA: MIT Press, pp. 289–90.

Warner, Andrew (2010). "The MP3.com Story – with Greg Flores". *Mixergy.com*. http:// mixergy.com/greg-flores-interview/ (accessed 18 November 2011).

Weiner, Joseph (2009). "Spinning in the Grave: The Three Biggest Reasons Music Magazines Like Vibe and Blender Are Dying". *Slate*. http://www.slate.com/id/2223381/ (accessed 1 May 2011).

Westergren, Tim (2012). "Pandora and Artist Payments". *Pandora: internet Radio*, 9 October. http://blog.pandora.com/pandora/archives/2012/10/pandora-and-art.html (accessed 11 October 2012).

White, Emily (2012). "The State of 360 Deals in 2012". *National Association of Record Industry Professionals*. http://www.narip.com/?p=8366 (accessed 11 December 2012).

Wikström, Patrik (2009). *The Music Industry*. Cambridge: Polity Press.

Williamson, John, and Martin Cloonan (2007). "Rethinking the Music Industry". *Popular Music* 26.2: 305–22.

Winner, Langdon (1978). *Autonomous Technology: Technics out of Control as a Theme in Political Thought*. Cambridge, MA: MIT Press.

Wood, James (1992). *History of International Broadcasting*. London: Peter Peregrinus.

Zickuhr, Kathryn (2011). "Generations and Their Gadgets". *Pew internet: Pew internet and American Life Project*. http://pewinternet.org/Reports/2011/Generations-and-gadgets/Overview.aspx (accessed 3 January 2012).

Discography

Adele (2011). *21*. XL.
Amanda Palmer (2011). *Amanda Palmer Goes Down Under*. Self-released.
Amanda Palmer (2011). 'Map Of Tasmania'. Self-released.
Arcade Fire (2004). *Funeral*. Merge/Rough Trade.
Bob Dylan (1969). *Great White Wonder*. Trademark of Quality.
Cher (1998). 'Believe'. WEA/Warner Bros.
Def Leppard (1987). 'Pour Some Sugar On Me'. Mercury.
Gorillaz (2010). *The Fall*. Parlophone.
Gotye (2011). 'Somebody That I Used To Know'. Eleven.
Head in a Jar (2011). *Atomic Circus*. Self-released.
John Butler Trio (2004). *Sunrise Over Sea*. Jarrah.
Jonathan Coulton (2006). 'Code Monkey'. Self-released.
Kutiman (2011). 'My Favourite Color'. http://www.youtube.com/watch?v=nIl4LkHYRkg
     (accessed 21 March 2012).
Leonard Cohen (2012). *Old Ideas*. Columbia.
Metallica (2000). 'I Disappear'. Warner Bros./Hollywood Records.
Nine Inch Nails (2007). *Year Zero*. Interscope.
Nine Inch Nails (2008). 'Discipline'. The Null Corporation.
Nine Inch Nails (2008). *The Slip*. The Null Corporation.
Nine Inch Nails (2008). *Ghosts I–IV*. The Null Corporation.
Radiohead (2007). *In Rainbows*. Self-released.
Saul Williams (2007). *The Inevitable Rise And Liberation Of NiggyTardust!* The FADER/
     Wichita Recordings/Sony.
Susan Boyle (2009). *I Dreamed A Dream*. Syco/Columbia.
Taylor Swift (2008). *Fearless*. Big Machine.
The Beatles (1967). 'Strawberry Fields Forever'. Parlophone/Capitol.
The Gregory Brothers (2010). 'Backin Up Song'. http://www.youtube.com/watch?v=zjY
     SERaXEGI (accessed 24 May 2012).
Travis Morrison (2004). *Travistan*. Barsuk.
Walk Off the Earth (2012). 'Somebody That I Used To Know'. http://www.youtube.com/
     watch?v=d9NF2edxy-M (accessed 14 May 2012).

Filmography

Justin Bieber: Never Say Never (2011). Directed by Jon M. Chu. Paramount Pictures.
King of Jazz (1930). Directed by John Murray Anderson. Universal Pictures.
The Piano (1993). Directed by Jane Campion. Ciby 2000.

Index

Note: All titles in italics are those of albums, unless identified as (book) or (film).